THE Mountains ARE Calling

The Mountains are Calling: 90 Devotions for Peace and Solitude

First Edition, March 2022

Published by:

Published by DaySpring, 501 Nelson Place, Nashville, TN 37214, USA. DaySpring is an imprint of HarperCollins Christian Publishing, Inc.

HarperCollins Publishers, Macken House, 39/40 Mayor Street Upper, Dublin 1, D01 C9W8, Ireland (https://www.harpercollins.com)

Written by: Bonnie Rickner Jensen
Cover Design by: Lauren Purtle

ISBN: 978-1-64870-330-0
ISBN: 978-1-4003-5870-0 (eBook)

Printed in China
26 27 28 29 30 CPP 9 8 7 6 5

THE Mountains ARE Calling

90 DEVOTIONS

for Peace + Solitude

DaySpring

Table of Contents

Purposefully Peaceful

Lord, through all the generations You have been our home! Before the mountains were created, before the earth was formed, You are God without beginning or end.

PSALM 90:1–2 TLB

There's peace in being home. In the morning it's where we open our eyes, take a deep breath, and gather courage for the day. In the evening it's where we get comfortable, exhale, rest, and restore. While there's no earthly home as comforting as having God at home in our hearts, there's nothing more peaceful than having the gift of both.

Home is the place we look forward to at the end of a day. It's where our favorite people are, where we keep things that are beautiful to us, and where we're safe being who we are, without hesitation. When our hearts are home to God, we invite Him to be all He wants to be in our lives, without reservation. He's there to be everything we need because that's who He is.

Our souls enjoy real peace when we give God a real place in our lives. We can't go through the motions every day hoping we don't run out of spiritual energy. Eventually, we will. It doesn't take a large quantity of time, but it does take some quality time. A "thank You" at the sight of a sunrise or with our first sip of coffee is a simple acknowledgement of God's goodness. It starts the day in a way that gets our attitude going in the right direction. Relationships are strengthened through little things. Gestures of love and appreciation build a strong foundation, and God enjoys them just like we do!

Today can be purposefully peaceful. We can set the tone right now. We can thank God for one thing . . . we can feel grateful for one person in our lives . . . we can decide to give one worry we've carried in our heart to the One who abides there and who is willing and ready to take it. We're so incredibly loved. We're so perfectly cared for. We're so daily delighted in. If we can imagine God wrapping His arms around us this moment, we can face every moment in our day peacefully, knowing He's here to be *everything* we need.

Dear God,

There's nothing in today that we can't do together. Give me peace for what's coming and spiritual strength to carry me through.

Riches for a Lifetime

Come before Him with thankful hearts.

PSALM 95:2 TLB

Good things go well together. Here are two good things we can do to nurture our essential and eternal relationship with God: (1) maintain a gratefulness journal and (2) set aside quiet time. They go perfectly together because we can do them simultaneously. When we sit down to write a few things we're grateful for every day, we think about the One who gives us all the good things in our lives. God takes center stage.

There aren't many things we can do that are as therapeutic as reflecting on our blessings and being thankful for them. Thankfulness keeps our focus on the positive and the good. It's a powerful deterrent for negative thoughts and the discouragement that comes with them. Thankfulness boosts our joy, activates our good memories, and energizes our faith. When we're grateful for what God has done, we get excited about what He's going to do!

It's going to be good. God said so, "I know the plans I have for you: prosperity, hope, and a future" (Jeremiah 29:11, author's paraphrase). There isn't a brighter promise than that, and it lights the way to one good thing after another. God won't give us perishable things, either. They'll be riches like peace, contentment, and joy. He'll give us a wealth of strength, grace, and compassion. The more thankful our hearts, the richer we become.

Even when life gets bumpy and our hearts get banged up along the way, we've got an eternal expense account that has *no limit*. We can draw from it twenty-four hours a day, seven days a week, fifty-two weeks a year, for the rest of our lives. Because we trust *that*, we can, "Be cheerful no matter what; pray all the time; thank God no matter what happens" (I Thessalonians 5:16–17 THE MESSAGE).

Dear God,

Thank You for every blessing I have in Jesus. There's nothing that enriches my life more.

Kindness in Creation

I am the Lord,
who exercises kindness.
JEREMIAH 9:24 NIV

When we exercise kindness, we emulate God. It brings His love into the world in the best way. It feels good when we're kind to others, and it feels good when kindness is shown to us. That good feeling comes from God's love moving through us and from His love being given to us. It's the *best* thing. Sometimes it's the bravest thing. And the one thing kindness always brings, and builds, is peace—inside us and around us.

It can seem like small kindnesses don't make big differences. But if we determine to be kind where we are, whenever and however we can, we seize every opportunity God gives us to lift the world to a better place. We also can't forget to slow down and let God show His kindness to us. It's something He loves to do.

His creation is *filled* with small kindnesses. The trickle of a woodland stream, the refreshing scent of pine, the bird foraging for food God provides, the perfect breeze, the spring blooms, the summer flowers, and the fall colors. His kindness fills the earth and restores us in a way that man-made things never will. We can surround ourselves with things that have beauty, but God *is* beauty. Every part of creation is part of Him, and it connects us to His love and kindness in a powerful way.

Set aside some time in the day to slow the pace and find a quiet place. Let God be kind to you through all that He created for you to enjoy. The thankfulness that comes with feeling connected to Him is one of the greatest ways to strengthen *our* kindness muscles. When we're deeply grateful for what He's given us, we're delighted at the chance to give to others—through small kindnesses inspired by God's beautiful, powerfully present love.

Dear God,

I'm thankful for the glory of Your creation and the reflection of Your kindness in every part of it.

A Life Filled with Good Things

He fills my life with good things! My youth is renewed like the eagle's!

PSALM 103:5 TLB

Some days it feels impossible to silence our minds or slow the pace of our lives. Our schedules, demands, and responsibilities are moving us through the months so fast that we barely have the strength at the end of a day to do any soul-searching or prayerful reflecting. Our heads hit our pillows, and the next thing we know our alarms are going off again.

In Psalm 4:4–5, David encourages us with these words: "Stand before the Lord in awe, and do not sin against Him. Lie quietly upon your bed in silent meditation. Put your trust in the Lord" (TLB). Silencing our minds and trusting God go hand in hand. But both can be hard to do. We live in a world where we're told to set goals and do what we have to do to reach them. In the flurry of getting from here to there, we tend to lose sight of the fact that sometimes God wants us to simply wait on Him.

Being silent and standing still go against the world's way of doing things, but God's way of doing things will get us to the best place at the perfect time. And our minds and bodies won't suffer all the unhealthy stress in the process.

God fills our lives with *good things*. If what we're doing, choosing, or racing to accomplish is fraught with stress, leaving little or no time to get quiet and do some soul-searching, there's a good chance God isn't in it. And it's a good time to realize we need to be still (let go) and let God resume the lead.

A lot of things in our lives can wait if we really think about it. What we want to get done isn't always what we *have* to get done. Silence allows God to come in and sort it out. He knows what love would do and what lies ahead—and if we trust the control to Him, it will *always* be good.

Dear God,

Make my heart sensitive to You and Your purposes for my life. Keep my priorities in line with the path You want me to follow.

Breathing Room

He's solid rock under my feet,
breathing room for my soul.
PSALM 62:2 THE MESSAGE

Reaching a spot on a hiking trail where the landscape opens up to a breathtaking view is a stop-in-your-tracks moment. It's one that inspires everything in us to say, "Thank God I'm alive!" It's a remarkable, memorable, and thoughtful experience. And it's incredibly good for our souls. God knew it would be, that's why He carved the hills and mountains so artistically. That's why He saturated nature with His beauty and love. And that's why we gain *so* much, physically and spiritually, by appreciating it.

In Romans 1:20, the apostle Paul explains that since the creation of the world, God's invisible attributes have been clearly seen and understood by the things that He made. His attributes are far above our ability to describe them adequately, but, without a doubt, love is the highest peak of them all. His love for us can't be pulled down by the weight of any wrongdoing, and it will never fall by way of unforgiveness. God's love for us isn't shaken by a single fear that we have or any number of times we falter in our faith. His love for us can't be toppled by our refusal to listen, our running from His will, or our resisting the reality of it.

God's love for us is insurmountable and unstoppable. There's nothing more solid under our feet and nothing more refreshing to our soul. He's the "breathing room" we need to survive the sometimes suffocating darkness in this world. Taking time to envelop ourselves in the things He made can prove to be the heavenly hug we need. Nature quiets the world and awakens our senses. It encourages us to see, hear, and praise Him. It opens our eyes to His all-encompassing love and His constant presence.

We have today. We can look for the moments love wants us to see. We can celebrate the truth that each one of us is a wonderful miracle created by God. We can be thankful His love for us is immovable and immeasurable—and every breathtaking thing He made is proof of it.

Dear God,

Thank You for the art of creation and the beauty You put in it to restore our souls and inspire us to see Your boundless love. You're so good!

Strength in Solitude

My strength comes from God, who made heaven, and earth, and mountains.

PSALM 121:2 THE MESSAGE

The mountain maker is our source of strength. Wow! There's nothing too hard for Him and no one more important to Him than *you*. It brings tremendous peace every day to know we won't face anything that He won't give us the courage to get through. But when worries and fears become loud in our minds, it's necessary for us to find a way to become quiet in our spirits.

Where we go to find quiet time is different for each of us, but it's hard to appreciate true quiet if we're not alone. We can enjoy time with our spouse or a good friend just being together in silence, but solitude is special. We connect with who we are and the One who made us in a deeper way, because they're intricately bound. We can't be secure in who we are without being one with our Creator. Solitude is imperative to staying grounded in our wonderfully unique and powerful purpose.

Our lives are meaningful *every day*. God loves us, and He loves the life He's given us. His greatest joy is seeing us live the abundant life found in Him. In Him we have mountain-making strength and mountain-moving hope. And nothing gets to us without going through His love first. Good is going to come from everything we surrender to Him. Hope is going to stand against anything that tries to diminish it. We can't let the world or the worry keep us from seeking the solitude and the strength our souls need.

Today is an invitation. It's a chance for us to respond to God's offer to strengthen us, fill us with peace, and fuel us with hope. If we can get alone for even a sliver of time to reconnect with the source of every good thing, we can take another step forward. We can be confident that we're valued and our purpose is irreplaceable. We are loved and *infinitely* cherished—and God is ready to move any mountain in our lives to reveal it.

Dear God,

My alone time with You is my strengthening solitude. Give me the courage I need to push through every worry and keep all my hope in You.

Nurturing Our Inner Peace

All things were made by Me; I alone stretched out the heavens. By myself I made the earth and everything in it.

ISAIAH 44:24 TLB

When we get quiet in a natural setting, the sound of everything around us is magnified while everything within us becomes peaceful. It's a great exchange. We hear the wind, the birds, the woodland animals, the water, and the leaves on the trees. The presence of God is permeating, pleasing, and peaceful. *All things were made by Him.* That's why spending time in the created world is healing for us *in every way.*

The rut of our daily routine needs a natural interruption once in a while. It's good for us to walk nature trails and hike or drive to scenic viewpoints to simply be still and take it all in. The fresh air revives us, the beauty inspires us, and the God who put it all in place restores us. It's impossible to be truly revived in a world overwhelmed with distractions. Notification dings, bright screens, news alerts, and social media scrolling are constant thieves of our time. Being proactive brings about peacefulness.

When we nurture our inner peace, we give our souls an anchor to hold us steady in the chaos of life. It's an assurance of God's strength in us and His love for us. These are unwavering things. These are the things that don't give way under stress or circumstances. His strength and love are the things that will secure our peace in any storm. Nurturing it is a necessity.

Whatever today brings, dig deep for the peace that holds everything in perspective and puts every care in God's hands. He'll give you strength. He'll love you perfectly. He'll hold you close. He'll ask you to *trust* Him. Try to find a tiny space of prayer for however long you can manage. The quiet will bring the connection. And the connection will be the restoration your soul needs.

Dear God,

Your strength and love ground me and bring the peace I need to get through the day. Remind me to get away whenever and however I can to simply be restored by the work of Your hands and the beauty around me.

Letting the Good Sink In

**You are good and do only good;
make me follow Your lead.**

PSALM 119:68 TLB

I wonder if we can imagine for a moment spending all our time with someone who is loving, kind, generous, gentle, patient, and forgiving. There are never any emotional outbursts or reactions, just slow, steady, quiet, and constant *good*. That's what we get in our times of alone time with God. It's so critical for our souls to be saturated in the goodness of who He is, often.

When we feel thankful, we reflect on the things God has done for us. We think about the times we trusted Him for help and He provided, the times He moved things into place at the right time, opened doors, or surprised us with a blessing we weren't expecting. God makes promises, and He faithfully fulfills them. Through the course of our lifetimes, the good things He does will be countless.

But it's equally wonderful to experience all God *is* through the simple act of seeking Him. It's calming to meditate on the pureness and perfection of His love for us. To be confident that it *never* becomes distant, never wanes, and refuses to change even when we make mistakes. When we react emotionally to disappointments or wait impatiently for our prayers to be answered, God's love is unmoved. It remains as strong and committed as it has ever been—a love that was securely in place before we took our first breath.

Solitude, reflection, and prayer allow God's goodness to sink in, to really settle into our souls. The calm we feel is the *good* in Him. It's the good always at work in our lives, drawn from the well of His infinite, inexhaustible love. We sometimes forget how short breaks from our busy lives do amazing things in us. We should stay mindful of it. The respites magnify the good in God and His unshakable love for us—giving the confidence we need to follow His lead.

Dear God,

Your love is my strength and confidence, my security and hope. You lead me to what is good, and my heart is thankful every day.

Becoming a Brave Believer

The Lord turn His face toward you and give you peace.
NUMBERS 6:26 NIV

It can be difficult to feel peaceful when life is hard. Tough seasons are part of our journey, but they sometimes compel us to seek and lean into what God has promised us. In John 14:27, Jesus said, "I am leaving you with a gift—peace of mind and heart! And the peace I give you isn't fragile like the peace the world gives. So don't be troubled or afraid" (TLB).

Peace of mind is the hurdle for most of us. Maybe that's why Jesus mentioned it first. It's where the thoughts come to battle, loaded with doubt, fear, and uncertainty. They try to uproot the good stuff as fast as we plant it. But the more we water the truth of God's promises, the deeper the roots go and the harder it is for *any* lie to pluck them out.

"I have told you all this so that you will have peace of heart and mind. Here on earth you will have many trials and sorrows; but cheer up, for I have overcome the world" (John 16:33 TLB); "His peace will keep your thoughts and your hearts quiet and at rest as you trust in Christ

Jesus" (Philippians 4:7 TLB); "What a wonderful God we have . . . who so wonderfully comforts and strengthens us in our hardships and trials" (II Corinthians 1:3–4 TLB).

The practical way to keep the weeds, or lies, from overtaking our minds is to keep *replacing* them with the truth. Words are life, and they're life-changing when spoken. God spoke every created thing into existence! Remember how often we read aloud as children? There's wisdom in doing it *now*. Peace will come by the power of truth, and peace of heart and mind is a gift God wants us to enjoy in full measure.

Let's read God's Word aloud today. Speak and *listen* to God's peace-giving words. Lean in and know His face is turned toward our troubled minds and hearts, and He's closer than He's ever been. Replace the lies that say we should be afraid, overwhelmed, and anxious with the truth that we're loved, held, and comforted. We can remove the bullying lies and become the brave believers—because *nothing* is impossible with God.

Dear God,

You're here to comfort me right now, and I trust You for the strength and courage I need to get through any and every circumstance in my life.

Our souls enjoy **real peace** when we give God a **real place** in our lives.

The Greatest Getaway

My peace I give you. I do not give to you as the world gives. Do not let your hearts be troubled.

JOHN 14:27 NIV

As ambitious, goal-setting humans, we like to look ahead. We like to plan, make lists, keep journals, and be in a "go-for-it" mode at all times. It makes us feel like we're living life to the fullest, and the world certainly encourages the *be better*, *do better*, *get more* mindset. Then there are the words of Jesus: "Get away with Me and you'll recover your life.. . . Keep company with Me and you'll learn to live freely and lightly" (Matthew 11:28–30 THE MESSAGE).

It's peaceful just to *read* those words. Imagine how we'd feel if we took Him up on that invitation every single day. If we'd focus as much on learning how to live lightly as we do on living successfully, we'd discover the importance of true rest. There's definitely a balance to strike between working hard and working *too* hard. The attitude of our hearts can help us maintain it: "Whatever you do, work at it with all your heart, as working for the Lord, not for human masters" (Colossians 3:23 NIV).

Working with a heart surrendered to the Lord will feel like a blessing and not a burden. He doesn't put anything heavy or ill-fitting on us—He fills us with purpose, gives us the gifts to succeed in it, and cheers us on along the way! When we start to feel burdened or burnt out, it's time to step back and get away with Jesus. It will restore the balance. Some time to seek His wisdom and search our hearts will reveal the changes we need to make. God's peace will be there to point us in the right direction.

Thankfully, God has gone ahead of us, so we can have peace today. We can make plans and lists. We can fill our journals with dreams—and we can trust Him with *all* of them. He's going to fill our lives with good things and answer our dreams with *more than we can imagine.*

Dear God,

I dedicate the work of my heart and hands to You and thank You for every good thing You have in store for me.

The Importance of Awe

The whole earth is filled with awe at Your wonders; where morning dawns, where evening fades, You call forth songs of joy.

PSALM 65:8 NIV

The created world exudes God's love for us. From mountain to ocean to everything in between, the majesty of God can be seen. Countless songs have been inspired by the work of God's hands. Hearts have been changed by the wonder of it. God draws us to Him and deepens our faith through the beauty of creation.

Spending time in nature is key to staying in touch with our authentic self, because there God surrounds us in a very tangible way—and He stitched together every thread of our being. Seeing the Grand Canyon for the first time has moved many, *many* visitors to tears. If you've been there, you've probably had a similar response. It can take your breath away and leave you speechless. The weather can change multiple times as you drive around the canyon. It's absolutely one of the "to God be the glory" wonders of the world.

Researchers have discovered that experiencing awe is good for us. Standing in awe of any part of God's handiwork puts our life in perspective and is incredibly humbling. It magnifies His goodness and fills us with gratefulness. The wonder of it energizes our faith in knowing *anything* is possible with Him. And the single reason for all He does for us, around us, and in us is His unconditional, unfailing love.

This is a day made for being grateful. It's a good day to look for awe-inspiring moments—in an unexpected kindness, a work of art, a stunning sunset, or the perfect form of a flower. God is here, and the earth is *filled* with His glory. What a *wonderful* way to be loved.

Dear God,

My heart is filled with gratitude for all You've made and given. Let my life be a clear reflection of Your presence in it, and remind me that miracles of Your love can be seen everywhere.

Shifting Priorities in the Silence

Search your hearts and be silent.
PSALM 4:4 NIV

Searching our heart is a valuable part of our quiet time. It gives us time to clear our thoughts, consider our pursuits, and reflect on what we spend most of our time doing. Is the majority of our time spent on things we value most? Are we doing enough to cultivate relationships, rather than climb ladders, gain followers, and seek promotions? It's a balance we won't strike without God's help.

If we ask Him, God will move our hearts to make wise choices and choose worthy ambitions. He'll direct our steps into the places, purposes, and people's lives that bring us fulfillment and joy, because He'll be at the center of it all. Striving and tension won't be part of His plan; instead, we'll be led with peace. Peace is one of the great indicators of God's involvement in our decisions. "Following after the Holy Spirit leads to life and peace" (Romans 8:6 TLB).

It can feel like nothing is getting done when we spend time in silence, but there are priceless things being done in us. We're decompressing, allowing our mind to settle, and giving our constantly moving thought life a much-needed slowdown. Once everything slows down, certain things start to surface. Our hearts and minds enjoy some true connection that results in priority shifting and God influencing. It's a win-win.

God doesn't want us to go ahead without Him. He wants to be *intricately* involved in everything we do. Love is His reason. He loves us more than anyone can or will, and He wants the absolute best for us. He wants us to get to the stuff that makes us feel joy deep down and gives us a defining purpose through and through. He's the only way to get there—and He's going to be cheering loudest when we do.

Dear God,

Show me the importance of being silent and hearing You more clearly. Light my path with Your loving wisdom and guidance every day.

The Peace in Perfect Love

When my heart is faint and overwhelmed, lead me to the mighty, towering Rock of safety.

PSALM 61:2 TLB

Is anything too hard for God? *Never.* Would He leave us alone or without the strength we need to overcome anything we face today? *Absolutely not.* Will we let *anything* steal our peace, knowing God is for us? *No way!* Replacing anxious thoughts with confident declarations can keep us from feeling overwhelmed. Peace comes on the heels of thinking about what perfect love would say to us. If the thought isn't something God would say, it's got to go!

Perfect love is the power of truth put into practice. Perfect love kicks out every fear that comes to take the place of faith. Perfect love lifts every hope God sends to carry us through. Perfect love erases every lie that tries to tell us God has stepped out of our lives. No matter what kind of wilderness it feels like we're walking through, love is in it with an endless river of strength behind it. And there's more beauty than we can imagine up ahead.

God wants us to experience the peace He gives in the midst of the overwhelming days and the seasons of waiting. Love doesn't leave when it gets hard. It faithfully leads with our best *always* at the center of its purpose. We can be at peace when things around us look like they're falling apart because we know God is putting them together for our good. That's why we put our trust in perfect love. That's why when our hearts are faint and overwhelmed, we choose to steer our thoughts in the direction of truth.

Truth says you are unique and wonderfully made. Truth says you are exactly where you should be on the way to what God has prepared for you. Truth says love emerges strongest in you when you feel weakest. And nothing in this world can defeat the strength that shows up on your behalf *every* time.

Dear God,

You are the strong, safe place my heart can take refuge in today. Fill my thoughts with Your truth and love, and give me renewed hope that every detail of my life is in Your hands.

Pause the Chaos

You answer us with awesome and righteous deeds, God our Savior, the hope of all the ends of the earth and of the farthest seas, who formed the mountains by Your power.

PSALM 65:5–6 NIV

Those who have climbed a mountain know the irreplaceable gifts in it. They learn about peace from mountains. The tranquility and calm at different stages of the challenge nourish the soul in a way no other experience can. And much like standing at the ocean, standing on a mountain gives us an appreciation of how small we are, while magnifying how *great* God is. It's beautifully humbling.

Nature is God's answer to so many things. Jesus encouraged us to watch the birds and consider the wildflowers if we ever question God's attentiveness to our needs and His faithfulness in meeting them. He put a promise in every rainbow and new mercy in every sunrise. He numbers the stars and calls them by name, orders the seasons, and holds the oceans in place. Is it any wonder we feel at peace in the natural world?

We need time to nurture peace in our lives. Being surrounded by God's handiwork feels like a pause in the chaos to relax with Him for a while. Every living thing is filled with His glory, and when we stop to notice and appreciate His creation, we get a renewed sense of how completely wonderful He is. Everything on this earth lives, moves, and has its being in Him, and He's aware of it all to the point of knowing when a sparrow falls.

Not a single part of our lives is overlooked. God is in every detail of our day and every facet of our future. He can be trusted with every outcome because His love outweighs every obstacle. He wants us to have peace, inside and out, and staying close to Him is how we get it. Go outside today to marvel at His presence in every living thing and to appreciate the soothing peace it brings.

Dear God,

Your presence in nature helps me nurture the peace I need. I know You see every detail of my life, and I trust You with every care I have. Thank You for being my constant comfort.

Slowing Down to See the Good Stuff

No doubt about it! God is good . . . But I nearly missed it, missed seeing His goodness.

PSALM 73:1 THE MESSAGE

We see more when we slow down. When we walk or ride a bicycle through a neighborhood we've driven through a hundred times, we see details we've never noticed before. Slowing our pace opens our eyes. It's a good reminder of how important it is to slow down—when we make decisions, when our schedules start to race out of control, and when we feel stress smothering the tranquility in our lives.

God is good at teaching us to use the brakes. "Rest in the Lord; wait patiently for Him to act" (Psalm 37:7 TLB). "God wants His loved ones to get their proper rest" (Psalm 127:2 TLB). "Relax and rest. God has showered you with blessings" (Psalm 116:7 THE MESSAGE). "Relax, everything's going to be all right; rest, everything's coming together; open your hearts, love is on the way" (Jude 1:2 THE MESSAGE).

If we keep sprinting through our days, we'll eventually get to a point when we stop and look back . . . but all we'll see is a blur. We'll realize we've missed too much of what was important and worried about too many things that weren't. God knows that rest helps us retain our balance. He knows that slowing down encourages us to see opportunities we're missing to love people, show kindness, and do things that light up the world.

God also puts our priorities right in front of us. Where we are in our lives, what we do every day, and the people we're here to love are perfectly in place. It's up to us to pace ourselves in a way that values what God has given us. We won't get a day back once it's spent. Slow down and make sure to see every detail of His kindness in your life at this moment. We never want to hurry past the good stuff.

Dear God,

Open my eyes to the priorities in my life. I don't want to miss the love and purpose in them. Give me wisdom in keeping everything in balance so I invest my time in the right pursuits and the most important things.

Silencing the Doubt

Trusting Me, you will be unshakable and assured, deeply at peace. In this godless world you will continue to experience difficulties. But take heart! I've conquered the world.

JOHN 16:33 THE MESSAGE

Is it possible for us to have peace in the midst of things that challenge our faith and fill us with doubt, or the noise of the news reports, or even the steady pressure of our everyday lives? The constant distractions can cause our thoughts to bounce around from one thing to another until we feel mentally exhausted and physically tired. It all feels nonstop, making peace seem unattainable.

The deep peace God gives is found in deeply trusting Him to take care of us. Doubt is very good at being a mental noisemaker. It sidetracks us from experiencing the peace that sustains our hope when life gets hard. Being alone can bring our hearts and minds back to a peaceful state, where we can tap into the love and truth that silences the doubt. A short walk boosts our sense of well-being and makes us happier. Anytime we get out of the rut we get refreshed enough to gain a little peace and go a little further.

God is *never* going to leave us. Any thoughts that suggest we've messed up too many times, taken too many wrong turns, or disappointed Him too many times are lies showing up to steal our peace. Jesus knows that trusting Him makes us unshakable and assured, so find a few moments of solitude to settle into that truth today. The peace you need won't be far behind.

Dear God,

Give me a deeper trust so I can live with a deeper peace. I know You have everything in my life worked out for my good and Your glory. I never need to doubt Your perfect love.

No Fear of Falling

He gives me the surefootedness of a mountain goat upon the crags. He leads me safely along the top of the cliffs.

PSALM 18:33 TLB

Mountain goats are amazing animals. They fearlessly navigate impossible rock faces and move along the cliffs with astounding agility and courage. They're designed for the task, but it doesn't diminish their extraordinary skill. David's comparison in Psalm 18 reveals how God has similarly equipped us to get through seemingly insurmountable situations in our lives. In the same way He gives a mountain goat surefootedness, He keeps our feet from slipping off the path of His will and leads us safely, one step at a time. We can move ahead without fear of falling, knowing God is with us.

Life is not without tests. There will be tough things, some far beyond our understanding. But if we courageously trust God, knowing He's leading us to a place where we'll be more confident in His love than ever before, the cliffs in life won't be daunting. We'll be braver and stronger. We'll feel safer and more secure. We'll be certain God is guiding us along the path *meant* for us.

When things we face feel scary, remember this: we'll never have to manage a single cliff in life without the firm grip of love holding us steady. Whatever it is, God knew it was coming, He sees how we'll get through, and He knows what's being cultivated in us. We're getting to the great stuff He has planned by trusting Him to build the good stuff *within* us. We're learning we can have peace in any situation. We're finding out that God's strength rises to meet every challenge to our faith and that hope won't let go even when we feel like we can't hold on any longer. *We get through because love won't give up on us.*

Today might look like a series of terrifying cliffs. It might look rugged, unpredictable, and impossible to manage. But *love*—taller than a mountain, deeper than an ocean, and wider than the sky—has you with both hands. You're not only going to get through, but you're also going to get braver, wiser, and more beautiful too.

Dear God,

You've got me! No matter what happens—the unexpected, the unplanned, the unnerving—I put all my trust in You. Every step is guided by love.

The Way to Perfect Peace

You're my place of quiet retreat; I wait for Your Word to renew me.

PSALM 119:114 THE MESSAGE

Just saying the words can bring peace: *God, You are my place of quiet retreat.* In a world fraught with fear, frantically increasing technology, and media platforms that push us further away from real connection, we need a real retreat. God is a real and reliable one.

So how do we get to a retreat that isn't a physical place? Words. "The very words I have spoken to you are spirit and life" (John 6:63 NLT). The peaceful, quiet retreat that God *is* can be reached by filling our hearts and minds with what God *says*. "Though the mountains be shaken and the hills be removed, yet My unfailing love for you will not be shaken nor My covenant of peace be removed" (Isaiah 54:10 NIV). "He will keep in perfect peace all those who trust in Him, whose thoughts turn often to the Lord" (Isaiah 26:3 TLB).

Words of truth are powerful, life-giving, *perfect peace* bringers. All God asks us to do is turn our thoughts to Him *often*. But there's no shortage of things competing for space in our mind. Worries want some room, to-do

lists want a fair share, self-inflicted expectations want to squeeze in, and comparison wants to demand a little corner of its own. Every bit of mental energy we give to those things pushes us away from our place of quiet retreat.

But a word of truth can push them back: "Don't worry about anything; instead, pray about everything; tell God your needs and don't forget to thank Him for His answers. If you do this, you will experience God's peace, which is far more wonderful than the human mind can understand" (Philippians 4:6–7 TLB).

Today can be as noisy or as quiet as you choose. If we give the right words priority in our minds, we can spend time in the quiet retreat of God's presence—and we can renew our strength, restore our hope, and rest in the peace of perfect love.

Dear God,

Your words are life to every part of my being. Thank You for the faithful retreat of Your love, where I find peace, courage, hope, and rest.

He formed the mountains by His mighty strength. He quiets the raging oceans and all the world's clamor.

PSALM 65:6-7 TLB

Solitude's Inspiration

We're in no hurry, God. We're content to linger in the path sign-posted with Your decisions . . .Through the night my soul longs for You. Deep from within my spirit reaches out to You.

ISAIAH 26:7–10 THE MESSAGE

We can forget how inspiring it is to be alone. Solitude is significant. It inspires us to thoughtfully reflect on all the moving parts of our lives. Being alone inspires heartfelt communication with God and gives us an opportunity to reconnect with who we are and what we dream of. Our true self comes to the forefront when the routines and responsibilities aren't demanding all our energy and attention.

Solitude is a breath of fresh air for our soul. It's like saying, "Hello, *you*. How is it *really* going?" It's also like hitting a release valve on the pressures the world imposes on us constantly: this is how to be a better wife, husband, parent, grandparent; this is what you do to look younger, stay healthy, get stronger, and live longer. The ads, advice, and personal improvement options are endless. But what do *we* feel is vital to our wellness? What do we hear God saying to us about the things we should focus on?

God takes His relationship with each of us personally. He longs for one-on-one time with us, any hour of the day or night. Prayer and solitude are ways for us to get answers to the questions we have about our *unique* purpose. Our life's journey isn't going to be identical to anyone else's. Our path will be marked with different experiences, failures, disappointments, and difficulties. Our heart will break for different reasons. Our growth will happen at a different pace. But if we trust God's leading, the path we take will be in perfect harmony with how He created us and what we're created to do.

Don't be in such a hurry today. Enjoy a bit of solitude. Open your heart and ask God to put you on the path of your purpose. It's where true fulfillment is and how we can be the greatest blessing to the greatest amount of people. That's God's deepest desire for all of us—because that's the purpose of love.

Dear God,

Reveal every way that I can be Your love today. Give me the patience to love my people and the people You bring across my path.

Losing Control to Find Peace

You will live in joy and peace. The mountains and hills, the trees of the field—all the world around you—will rejoice.

ISAIAH 55:12 TLB

What are the best ways to find peace? Externally, we hike a forest trail, kayak a quiet waterway, walk the beach, bike the countryside, or climb a mountain. Internally, we trust God. The latter is straightforward and simple, but it can be a lot harder for us to do. As humans in a fast-moving world, where conveniences, quick results, and instant gratification are at an all-time high, we can fall into the habit of taking control rather than trusting God.

When things in our life start to flare up or fall apart, we instinctively start planning solutions. How can I fix this problem? How can I handle this conflict? How can I get through this without crawling into bed and pulling the covers over my head? The truth is, and thankfully, we just need to go to God and surrender the struggle. It's good to be completely transparent with our feelings and fears, even though He knows them all. The honesty is for our benefit. We get better at letting Him take the controls when it gets easier for us to confess how much we can't do it alone.

God knows that realizing we need Him is the highest hurdle we'll cross in getting to the perfect peace He alone can give. We need God. Every day, in every decision, and in every battle we face. No one loves us as much or comes to our side as fast or as faithfully. The One who carved mountains and separated oceans is waiting for us to simply *ask* for the help we need, and then to trust Him with the wisest, best, and most loving response.

There's peace for today. We can have it outside in His creation, and we can have it inside through His grace. Nothing is too hard for Him and *anything* is possible *with* Him. When we trust Him with all our heart, we have peace no matter what we face—and we know His love will give exactly what we need.

Dear God,

I trust You with every detail of my life today. Take all my worries and take away my desire to control the things only You can.

Back to a Peaceful State

In one hand He holds deep caves and caverns, in the other hand grasps the high mountains. . . . His hands sculpted Earth!

PSALM 95:4 THE MESSAGE

The hands that sculpted earth sculpted you. The desires God put in your heart are designed to point you in the direction of your purpose. The gifts you have are your guides. The place you're at right now is part of the plan. Peace is the presence of God leading you. Peace is a powerful signal that you're on the path He chose for you, one lined with love, lessons, and the lives you're meant to touch. Your life has *infinite* value every single day.

When it starts to feel like the majority of the time we're overwhelmed and less of the time we're at peace, it's time to pause. Peace and solitude work together. When we get alone, our hearts and minds have a chance to get back to a peaceful state. God designed us with such detail and care. He never wants us to feel overcome by life and its demands. He wants to be an intricate part of everything we do, so His peace can calm, comfort, and direct us.

Problems can become mountains of worry when we don't surrender them to God.

He's always working the pieces of our lives together in ways that grow our faith and deepen our trust in Him. Even when we don't understand the timing or why it's so difficult, God loves us tenderly through it all and holds us closer than ever. Our broken heart beckons His embrace.

God's faithfulness brings beauty from ashes and joy from any depth of sadness we suffer. His earth-sculpting hands have the power to move any mountain in our lives when we hold on to our faith. We can win our tug-of-war with doubt if we slow down, seek solitude, and stay at peace. God is leading the way with love that will *never* fail.

Dear God,

My life is in Your hands. Carry me when my strength is spent, calm my fears, and give me peace in Your loving lead.

One Unique Life

May He grant you according to your heart's desire, and fulfill all your purpose.

PSALM 20:4 NKJV

Times of prayer should never be an option for us. Getting alone and quiet with the intent of hearing God is the most encouraging, energizing, and edifying thing we can do. Our souls are moved when we move closer to our purpose. And there is a deep satisfaction in being confident about how we're created and why the desires of our hearts are what they are.

God has *everything* to do with discovering what we're in this world to do. He saw our life in its entirety before we took our first breath. It's amazing to think about. Who better to turn to and trust completely? We need only to look back at what He's done, how He's shown Himself in unquestionable ways and small miracles, and how we've grown in the wake of them. He has so much more for us to do. Each of us is an invaluable, irreplaceable part of His plan.

Our purpose is connected to the passions God put in our hearts. Our gifts—the unique traits we have and what ignites a fire in us—will be engaged in our life's journey. Not one of our paths will be exactly the same. They might run side by side, intersect, or go in completely different directions, but they all lead to the glory of God. That's why we're here. We're here, most importantly, to *love as He loves*. The good life is never about us or what we gain or accomplish; it's how good we are at loving the people God puts in our lives.

Our purpose for today is perfectly bound to the One who is love, life, light, and kindness. All the things that make this world beautiful are found in Him. We're here to learn to trust Him with our one, extraordinary, unique life and to pour it out with love and grace.

Dear God,

I trust You with the plans You have for me. I know they begin and end with love, and every desire in my heart leads to a life lived for Your glory.

The Path to Peacefulness

You chart the path ahead of me and tell me where to stop and rest. Every moment You know where I am.

PSALM 139:3 TLB

We all have different things we like to do to relax, unwind, and feel at peace. It might be finding a comfy, quiet place to read, sitting in a coffee shop having a favorite brew, taking a walk, cooking, or working in the garden. The path to peacefulness is often doing the simple things we enjoy. That's why it's important to do them.

A lot of days we slight the stuff we like to do because of the stuff we have to do. We find ourselves falling into bed feeling completely wiped out. And too much of the time that's when our minds start revving up. We go through the next day mentally, or worse, we go over past days that can't be changed. All of it steals the peace our minds and bodies need.

We have to be careful not to make it too difficult to create little pockets of peace throughout the day. We think we have to set apart a chunk of time to find the peacefulness that comes with simple joys. But it doesn't have to be on the schedule. Stepping away from our routine for even a few minutes can make a big difference. It doesn't take long for God to restore us through a few deep breaths, a quick clearing of our mind, some fresh air, and a strength-seeking prayer.

God is for us. *Always.* He wants us to trust Him, pay attention to the signals our body gives when we've gone too long without a peaceful pause, and to remember we're created for the peace we find in simple joys. It's in those moments that we feel grateful, fully loved, and completely connected to the gift of life He gives.

Dear God,

Remind me today that You created every detail of who I am and the things that bring me joy are paths to peacefulness and time with You.

The Peace that Protects

A heart at peace gives
life to the body.
PROVERBS 14:30 NIV

We feel better when our hearts are at peace. Our bodies follow the lead of our hearts, minds, and emotions. Philippians 4:6–7 says, "Do not be anxious about anything, but in every situation, by prayer and petition, with thanksgiving, present your requests to God. And the peace of God, which transcends all understanding, will guard your hearts and your minds in Christ Jesus" (NIV).

It takes time to trust God completely and get to the point of living with a peaceful heart every day, regardless of what happens. We don't get there quickly. We stumble over holding on to worry until we're stressed out, we struggle with waiting on God, we trip over trying to control outcomes, and the list goes on. We all have our personal variations, and we all understand that peace is a gift from God worth receiving. It comes with priceless rewards like health, joy, and a good night's sleep.

Pray about everything. That's the prerequisite for the peace of God. This isn't the peace we get from finding a quiet place to think or taking a long walk on the beach. God's peace is the kind our minds will *never* understand. It's the peace that *protects* our hearts and minds—the peace that stands guard against anything and everything life throws at it. God's peace gives *life*.

Sustained peace takes disciplined thoughts. "Whatever is true, whatever is noble, whatever is right, whatever is pure, whatever is lovely, whatever is admirable—if anything is excellent or praiseworthy—think about such things" (Philippians 4:8 NIV). It's as easy and as challenging as that. If we ask, God will help us direct our thoughts toward good things and redirect those that aren't good. And this is always a good go-to: "We are able to hold our heads high no matter what happens and know that all is well, for we know how dearly God loves us" (Romans 5:5 TLB).

Dear God,

Everything in my life is in Your hands. Help me let go and trust You with the things I'm worried about today. Guard my heart and mind with Your peace and love.

Peace Rooted in Love

Even if I had the gift of faith so that I could speak to a mountain and make it move, I would still be worth nothing at all without love.

I CORINTHIANS 13:2 TLB

Everything we do in this world is reduced to nothing if love isn't our highest goal. We'll fall short countless times, but grace will carry us back to the starting line again and again. Emotion and exhaustion will get the best of us, and words that shouldn't be spoken will be said. Anger will be left to simmer until wrong actions boil over. Life is hard, our patience runs out, and the bad news keeps coming. It feels like love has stepped into the shadows while fear, frustration, and falsehood have taken center stage.

How do we put love in the spotlight when the headlines dim our hope every day and the thing getting all the attention is the pervading darkness? Collectively, *we keep loving*. We keep seeing the best in people and believing the best about them. We keep trusting that peace is rooted in love, and the One who *is* love is the way to find true peace. When we cast seeds of God's love, we plant light everywhere. Before long, the world will get a lot brighter. Spread the love, stay grounded in peace, and hold on to hope. We can do this!

Every new day is another opportunity to trust God, be at peace, and bring the love. Even small gestures matter in a big way. There's no such thing as an insignificant act of love. God can do miracles through our lives. Let Him! Love is powerful proof of God's presence. Love perpetuates peace and highlights hope. It does every good thing that can be done . . . right now, where we are, through every chance we're given.

Dear God,

I want love to be my highest priority. Make me a willing vessel of Your miracle-working love today. I'll rest in Your perfect peace and be light in a dark world.

Confident and Calm

Trusting Me, you will be unshakable and assured, deeply at peace.

JOHN 16:33 THE MESSAGE

How differently do we feel in a tense environment versus a peaceful one? Sometimes without realizing it we become stressed, and without meaning to, we react negatively. We find ourselves becoming critical, giving short answers, and carelessly hurting others with our words. Maintaining our inner peace can positively influence anything we face. That's why we should be deliberate about cultivating it every day.

Prayer is key. Asking God to help us be aware of our need for His strength and love at all times will help us keep our cool at all times. Instead of being affected by what's happening around us, we can be a calming presence to those around us when we ask for and receive God's wisdom. We can trust Him to hold us steady, lead us faithfully, and show us how to respond peacefully. When we rely on Him, we reflect His love. Love is *always* the best response.

Today might not go smoothly. When dealing with people anything is possible. We might find ourselves in the middle of something we didn't expect, and it might challenge our patience, our peace, and our prayer. But trusting God in the moment makes us unshakable in the moment. He never leaves our side or the situation we're in. He's well able to give us the deep peace that Jesus promised. Being confident in Him keeps us calm in every circumstance. And calm creates peace.

Dear God,

I need Your strength today. I want Your deep and abiding peace to guide my words and actions to a loving response. I surrender every situation to You and the wisdom of Your perfect heart.

The Light through Any Storm

God makes His people strong. God gives His people peace.

PSALM 29:11 THE MESSAGE

During a mountain climb the weather can change quickly, presenting many different and dangerous conditions to overcome. Being prepared for them is critical to succeeding and, more importantly, to surviving. Likewise, our lives are ever-changing and full of challenges. We can experience things that make climbing out of bed in the morning feel like an impossible feat. Sudden storms in life are hard and heartbreaking, but thankfully we never have to navigate them alone.

Overcoming *anything* is possible for us because Jesus gave everything He could to make it so. The way we get through is by clinging to the peace He won on our behalf. The way we keep going is by being confident of His perfect sacrifice and God's perfect love. They're both beyond our ability to comprehend, but they're more absolute and powerful than anything that can come against us.

You have all the strength of heaven behind you today. You don't have to feel like there's something else to do, another goal to reach, or a higher hurdle of faith to clear. God doesn't expect you to prove or provide anything. You're covered. You're carried. You can be confident that the overcoming is done, and you can have peace in any storm.

There will be calm again. There will be days that feel like sunshine on your face and a canoe ride down a quiet stream. There will be deeper joy and braver faith. Every good thing God brings from what we go through will emerge to heal and comfort us. He's making us strong and giving us peace in the process—and love is holding us every step of the way.

Dear God,

Your love is the light that leads me through any storm. I trust the sureness of it and the strength in it. I have peace in knowing Your faithfulness never fails.

Refreshment for the Faint

I will refresh the weary and satisfy the faint.

JEREMIAH 31:25 NIV

Worry can come with weariness. When we go too many days without prioritizing the time with God we need, we get run-down. Then we let stress, worry, and the weight of life run over our courage and hope. We can't let that happen! God is at the ready to refresh us and renew our strength. He's waiting for us to turn off the world and tune into His presence. Love will be there. Peace will be there. Wisdom will be there. *Whatever we need* will be there.

The wonderful thing about dedicated time with God is the way it slows time. What a gift. Most of our days are spent following routines planned out in increments of minutes and hours, and often we run out of them before we get everything done. The undone gets moved into the next twenty-four hours, and so on, and so on, until our days and weeks leave too little time for the *alone with God time* we need.

Quiet time breaks the cycle. It takes our eyes off the clock. And it's surprising how *little* it takes to feel refreshed and revived. Maybe we've complicated how simple it can be to work God time into our days. It truly can be going into a room, shutting the door, closing our eyes, and taking a few deep breaths. It can be stepping outside and feeling immediately thankful for the fresh air. It can be putting the phone on silent and staring out the window for a few moments just to clear our thoughts.

Today is a good day to start making those minutes with God a priority. It's going to take practice. It's going to take persistence. But the gifts it holds are worth receiving. The moments we spare are moments we surrender to God's loving care. His love wants what is best for us, and it's what we need most. Take a little time to soak it in.

Dear God,

I know being alone with You is the best
way to savor the goodness You offer.
Help me stay consistent in making time
for the refreshment You give.

Solitude
is a breath of
fresh air for
our souls.

Love in Every Step

Embrace peace—don't let it get away!

PSALM 34:14 THE MESSAGE

Peace is different in the mountaintop seasons of life. We make it through difficult valleys and are able to look back over the experience with a clearer perspective. We see things we couldn't see while we were in the middle of them, when it was darkest and we were at our lowest point. The climb is never easy. It's a hard-fought journey to get to a higher, more mature place of humility and surrender. But the view is *always* worth it.

We see God's love in *every* step we've taken. We see there was light guiding our way even when we didn't have the strength to look up. We see how God used everything we went through to help us grow, and we see the wisdom in His choices. We might not understand it all, but we understand it more fully. What's best for us is the greatest desire of God's heart. We wouldn't choose the trials, but God knows the rewards that are coming. He wants us to enjoy them *all*. He wants us to have strength, peace, confidence, joy, and hope more abundantly than ever before.

The peace of God is a little sweeter and a lot more securely rooted beyond the struggle. We're braver in our faith and we trust Him in a deeper way. And when we face another valley, our peace isn't easily shaken or taken. We'll be confident that, in time, God will reveal yet another aspect of the indescribable beauty of His love.

Sustained, sweet, secure peace is something we can have in God alone. It's the kind of peace that promises everything is going to be okay no matter what, because God is in control no matter what it looks like. The peace God gives is ours to embrace today—with both arms and all our heart—*wherever* we are on the love-guided journey of our life.

Dear God,

My steps are ordered by You, and the seasons of my life are in Your hands. Give me peace in every part of my journey, and let my heart surrender to Your wise and loving choices every day.

Time to Reflect and Reset

Get away with Me and you'll recover your life. I'll show you how to take a real rest.

MATTHEW 11:28 THE MESSAGE

Gratitude bubbles to the surface in times of reflective rest. It's one of the best benefits of spending time away from the regular routine of our lives. We sit and think. We pause and pray. We reflect and reset. All the things we're thankful for come forward to be fully appreciated. We realize we've been rushing past them too many days without stopping to give gratitude its proper place. We discover *again* how meaningful rest is in filling our hearts with praise.

God is the giver of every good thing in our lives. *Real rest* is good. Recovering a life of peace and contentment from one that has us feeling overworked and overtired is *really* good. Jesus has the right-fitting life for us. It frees us from worry and lifts everything that weighs us down. Knowing how He lived in this world is the way we learn how to live in this world. He trusted God completely and surrendered to Him fully. Jesus knew the depth, width, and the dependability of the Father's love. And He proved that it will *never* fail.

We're living at a time when it's hard for us to get away as often as we need to get away. That's why we have to make the most of the fragments of rest and downtime we can work in to our day, *every* day. It's too beneficial to be neglected. If we stay mindful of the words of Jesus, we'll stay more aware of our need for rest: "Come to Me and I will give you rest—all of you who work so hard beneath a heavy yoke. Wear My yoke—for it fits perfectly—and let Me teach you; for I am gentle and humble, and you shall find rest for your souls; for I give you only light burdens" (Matthew 11:28 TLB).

Dear God,

Trusting You lifts the heaviness that life can bring. Teach me to rest in You, and let Your love guide everything I do.

Calm at All Times

A calm, cool spirit keeps the peace.

PROVERBS 15:18 THE MESSAGE

It's hard to remain calm in every situation we face. Some days life can feel like a crash course in staying calm and exercising patience—there's a test at every turn! We're short with the people we love, we're long on grumbling, and we're tired of holding it all together. We just need a little time to fall apart and cry.

It's okay to feel that way, and it's okay to have those cries. They're sometimes the best way to get a good soul-washing. It can help clear the haze that's built up from carrying too much worry and having too little time alone. We need quiet time with God to calm the storm within us—the one that can cause us to drift away from the source of our strength, patience, wisdom, and peace. We find ourselves out in the rough, stressful waters of weariness, and we say things that aren't kind and do things that aren't loving.

Finding calm fosters peace. God is our calm at all times, in any test, and through every storm. Staying close to Him is the way to keep our cool. When we're connected to the overwhelming gentleness of His love and compassion, we reflect it. We become more like Him: "I am slow to anger and filled with unfailing love and faithfulness. I lavish unfailing love to a thousand generations" (Exodus 34:6–7 NLT).

Make an effort to carve out a few minutes alone with God today. Lean into and learn the gentleness and patience you want to show to those around you. Do it because God's love for us is every answer to every need, and He wants us to get wrapped up in it *every chance we get.*

Dear God,

Give me a calm spirit and the patience to give a gentle, loving response in any situation. Teach me to be more loving and wise with my words and actions.

Glory on Display

His glory towers over the earth and heaven!

PSALM 148:13 NLT

A mountain climb offers breathtaking beauty and a rare, unique glimpse of God's glory on earth. There are flowers and trees growing in seemingly impossible conditions; dramatic rock faces sculpted by time, elements, and the hand of our Creator; cascading waterfalls; and snowy peaks. The splendor of God is on full display in the mountains, and it fills us with fascination and wonder. It's a place that draws our deepest praise and highest honor for who He is and what He's done.

Our souls need the nurturing, healing gifts that nature gives—we were created by the *same* heart and hands. God is the giver of life and the creator of all we see. It's no surprise that we feel centered, relaxed, refreshed, and restored when we spend time in God's glorious creation. *God is in every part of it.* When we think of our favorite times of closeness to God, we often think of times we've spent outdoors. Whether it be planting a garden in our backyard, on a camping trip, boating, hiking through a forest, climbing a hillside, or taking a walk through a beautiful park, being outside is *great* for our inside!

Making space for quiet time is a challenge we all face. There's always so much to do. Our lives are full, for good reasons and in good ways. But unless we determine to schedule time to get out and away from the noise, demands, and hectic pace of our everyday lives, we could miss the glory of God that is on display in our own backyards.

We can be deliberate about restoring our soul today. We can make a plan for a weekend getaway or do some getting out close to home. Whatever time we spend appreciating the glory of God, by being saturated in nature, will be worth the effort. He loves to see us enjoy nature—it's a vibrant, beautiful, and miraculous expression of His goodness to us.

Dear God,

I praise You because I'm wonderfully made, and I'm surrounded by the glory in everything You've created. Thank You for restoring me through the work of Your hands. Your goodness is the joy of my heart.

The Bigger Picture

His compassions never fail. They are new every morning.

LAMENTATIONS 3:22–23 NIV

When our morning unfolds peacefully, we feel ready to move into the day with confidence. Our attitude is positive, our mood is relaxed, and our patience is longer than usual. God would love for us to live every day peacefully—letting Him carry the worry, trusting Him when the unexpected happens, and believing He'll meet all our needs, no matter what.

Even when it isn't peaceful around us, we can have it within us. Peace is a deep-seated trust that God is in control. He's guiding us to a good place, working in our lives for the best outcome, and giving us an even bigger picture of His amazing, unstoppable love. The peace God gives doesn't depend on circumstances. While they change continually, He never does. He's our perfect Father even when things aren't coming together as fast as we'd like them to. When the wait is long, love is still working on our behalf.

The peace that passes understanding is ours every morning when we open our eyes. It's rooted in compassion that won't fail and love that will never run out. Whether or not things go smoothly or exactly as planned when the day starts, our inner peace can hold steady. It's strong and dependable. It's promised and powerful. It's God's presence in every situation.

Love has gone before us today. It surrounds us with grace and God's goodness, the things that can't let us down and won't let us go. All we have to do is extinguish our doubt and energize our faith. "We are able to hold our heads high no matter what happens and know that all is well, for we know how dearly God loves us" (Romans 5:5 TLB). "I will praise the Lord no matter what happens. I will constantly speak of His glories and grace" (Psalm 34:1 TLB). If we trust the truth and offer the praise, we can make this a *peace-filled* day.

Dear God,

Your compassion was new with the sunrise, and Your love will give me the strength I need today. I trust You, and my heart is at peace no matter what the day brings.

Carving Out Quiet Time

Never forget Your promises to me . . . for they are my only hope. They give me strength in all my troubles; how they refresh and revive me!

PSALM 119:49–50 TLB

We thrive in calmness. We think clearly when we're calm. We're more likely to act and react lovingly when we're calm. We're most likely to follow the still, small voice of God within us when we're calm. One of the best ways to maintain calm in our lives is to carve out the quiet time we need.

God gets to the deepest parts of us when we get silent, and that's where we need our strength to be shored up. That's where we want Him to plant truth, give us confidence in His love, and reveal the power of the grace we walk in every day. We tend to spend our alone time thinking about what God has done in our lives. We think about the way He came through when we felt hopeless or the way He taught us through an experience—and it felt like *love*, not condemnation. He's gentle and kind, and who He is never changes.

Meditating on the goodness of God can keep us anchored, emotionally and spiritually. The more time we spend letting our hearts and minds dwell on His faithfulness, the more we see that His love is constantly active in our lives. There's no hint of turning in Him. He's always with us, knowing what's coming and giving us the strength to face it. He doesn't forget His promises to us, and He won't fail to keep them.

Go through today with a calm, carefree spirit. There's nothing on the way that God won't give you the grace to handle. His joy is our strength, so enjoy the good things He brings and lean on Him if there are some not-so-good things. His love covers it all—and that's more than enough comfort to give us courage and keep us calm.

Dear God,

I'll think of Your faithfulness and the love
in every promise You give. In You alone
I'm strong and hopeful, carefree and calm.

Divinely Ordered Downtime

You spoke, and at the sound of Your shout the water collected into its vast ocean beds, and the mountains rose.

PSALM 104:7–8 TLB

The majesty of the mountains inspires us to think about the greatness of God. At the sound of His voice, in obedience to His words, ocean waters flowed into place and mountains rose. All of creation is breathtaking proof of His divine nature and eternal power. The natural world renders it impossible to deny the vastness of His love, the depth of His grace, the beauty of His character, or the glory due Him.

We don't have to go to the grand things in nature to see the awesomeness of God. We can be in awe watching a bumblebee pollinate a flower, growing a garden from seeds, or seeing the perfection in a dew-covered spider web. His gifts to us are everywhere. The intricacy in the smallest thing is as miraculous as the stars being named, numbered, and suspended in the heavens. God loves us more than *any* other thing He created. We're His masterpiece and the joy of His heart.

There will be days when we don't feel like a miraculous, magnificent, *masterpiece* created by an awesome, amazing God. But those days don't make it less true. We're here on purpose and we're part of His perfect plan. We can be trial-weary, run-down from routine, or just plain tired from being our best for the people we love. But we should always remember the God who knit us together will be there to hold us together.

It's hard to keep bringing the love if we don't take time to bask in the love we're given. We need quiet, rest, and some divinely ordered downtime (Matthew 11:28). God will strengthen us from the inside out. He'll remind us that love is working things out for our highest good. He'll renew our confidence, and maybe, if we're spending quiet time outside, He'll make His presence known in the beauty of the miracles around us.

Dear God,

Creation reveals Your power, presence, and love, refreshing my soul in countless ways. Help me be sensitive to my need for quiet time with You.

Rest in the Truth

Ask where the good road is, the godly paths . . . Travel there, and you will find rest for your souls.

JEREMIAH 6:16 TLB

In this world, we need stress-subsiding strategies. Better put, we need stress-*squashing* strategies! We need to learn how to decompress after a tough day and give our souls the peace they crave. God is our guaranteed stress remover, but we might have a hard time letting go. Stress is often connected to worry, and our minds and bodies can become overwhelmed by it without us realizing it's happening.

God simply did not create us to carry the weight of worry. It's a heaviness that drives us away from our purpose and into the world's way of doing things. The world will tell us to maintain control and composure, offer five ways to fix the problem, and make us believe that God is a distant, not-always-dependable option. In John 14:27, Jesus said, "I am leaving you with a gift—peace of mind and heart! And the peace I give isn't fragile like the peace the world gives. So don't be troubled or afraid" (TLB). In truth, God is the *only* option for real peace.

Being troubled by anything that may or may not happen in the future or shamed by mistakes we've made in the past are *sure* ways to sabotage the peace of God in our lives. God has no memory of our mistakes. We're the ones who have a hard time forgetting. But that's how guilt works. It's a thief of our time and the things God has for us to do.

Truth erases the guilt and ushers in the grace. Truth showers us with love and permeates our hearts, souls, and minds with the peace of God. Truth wipes out the worry and smothers the stress that comes with it. Travel the path of truth today and find rest for your soul for the rest of your life. God says, "I will be your God throughout your lifetime—until your hair is white with age. I made you, and I will care for you. I will carry you along and save you" (Isaiah 46:4 NLT).

Dear God,

I surrender my worry to You and ask You to replace the stress I feel with the security of Your love and care. Keep my heart and mind on the path of truth.

Healing, Hope, and Our Highest Praise

I have calmed and quieted my soul.

PSALM 131:2 NKJV

Sometimes it's good to silence the phone, the Bluetooth speaker, and the conversation. It gives us a chance to listen to the sound of the wind in the trees. It allows us to hear the cardinal's evening song—its pure, clear notes *must* be praise and thanksgiving. It did nothing to earn or deserve the provision it was given for the day, but God didn't hesitate to give it. He's good all the time. And He's the life in *every* created thing.

Creation urges praise from the deepest part of us. Nothing else reveals Him in the same way, maybe because everything He created before us, He created *for* us. Its purpose is to nurture and inspire us and, most importantly, to express the magnitude of His love. Life is a *gift*, and it comes from God alone.

It's incredibly healthy for us to slow down and simply observe, listen, and breathe. It's a wonderful way to praise

God for all He's given us to enjoy. While we can make our houses cozy, beautiful, and relaxing, they can't compare to healing power of His handiwork or the way creation nurtures and refreshes us. God is our healer, our hope, and the focus of our highest praise—it only takes a little time in His glorious creation to reignite every one of those truths within us.

The next time you calm and quiet your soul, make a point of finding a favorite place to do it. Whether it be on your patio, at a city park, or under a tree in the backyard, stare at the sky, breathe in the fresh air, and relish God's gift of hope and healing. His presence is tangible in the beauty of nature—so carefully designed to reflect His sweet love.

Dear God,

Thank You for the endless gifts of Your love and life in all You've created. I'm grateful for Your calm, peaceful presence in Your creation and the healing it brings.

The Safest Place to Be

My help and glory are in God—granite-strength and safe-harbor-God—So trust Him absolutely . . . God is a safe place to be.

PSALM 62:8 THE MESSAGE

Today, pray for the *"it-doesn't-matter"* kind of peace. *It doesn't matter* if things don't go as planned; God's plan will prevail without fail and His plan is best. *It doesn't matter* if the news isn't what we hoped for; our hope is in God alone and His love won't falter. *It doesn't matter* if the wait is longer than expected; God's timing is perfect, and He sees the whole picture and orchestrates the most loving outcome. We can know that God is a safe place to be, and we can trust Him *absolutely*.

Things happen in our lives that seem insensitive and unfair. When they do, it's hard to rise above our feelings and stand in faith. But it's possible and doable if we make truth, peace, and faith our covering. One way to do that is to, "Use every piece of God's armor to resist the enemy whenever he attacks, and when it is all over, you will still be standing up" (Ephesians 6:13 TLB). God will give us the strength to keep standing. He'll be our refuge when we need rest. He's our help, as sure as the mountains stand tall and the oceans stay in place. It doesn't matter what comes—our peace comes from the One who holds the world in His hands.

"The earth is the LORD's, and everything in it, the world, and all who live in it" (Psalm 24:1 NIV) means we're never out of His sight or separated from His love. It's a love beyond explanation or understanding. It's a love that means God is always for us, never against us or indifferent to what we're going through. His compassion so outweighs our doubts, downfalls, and disappointments, that there isn't *anything* we could do to push it away.

God is working in our lives today. Love is in every decision He makes. Trust is our peace, and hope is our confidence. It doesn't matter what we see; it matters who is holding us steady—and to Him we matter more than we can fathom.

Dear God,

Give me the peace that passes understanding today, to keep my heart and mind safe in You. Your love is in control.

Find a quiet, secluded place so you won't be tempted to role-play before God. Just be there as simply and honestly as you can manage. The focus will shift from you to God, and you will begin to sense His grace.

MATTHEW 6:6 THE MESSAGE

Praise and a Sunset

From the rising of the sun to
the place where it sets,
the name of the Lord is to be praised.

PSALM 113:3 NIV

Watching the sunset only takes a few minutes of our evening, but it can be a precious few minutes of praise. We appreciate another day of life and think about how meticulously God composes everything on earth and in the heavens. Every part of it is in beautiful, astounding harmony. We're awestruck and peaceful at once.

Being awestruck can sustain divine joy in us. Marveling at the wonders of creation reminds us how good God is and how amazing it is that we have His full attention at all times. We praise Him: "O Lord my God, many and many a time You have done great miracles for us, and we are ever in Your thoughts. Who else can do such glorious things? No one else can be compared with You" (Psalm 40:5 TLB).

There's no comparison to the One who loves us best, brings out the best in us, and wants the best *for* us at all times. It's impossible to fully comprehend. But the deep-down joy nurtured by a sense of wonder is priceless and worth pursuing. If we need to relearn how to do it, we need only to spend time with a child. Wonder is heightened in children. Their hearts are filled with it. And the kingdom of heaven belongs to those with hearts like theirs.

Look for moments of wonder in your life today. When you see something beautiful, when someone is kind, when the sunlight shines into the room and makes everything brighter, remember God is thinking about you in those same moments—and His awesome, endless love is there. There is joy in His presence and strength in His joy. Spend some time praising Him!

Dear God,

Restore in me a sense of awe and help me stay present in the moments to see Your presence throughout my day.

Take a Break

Hour by hour I place my days in Your hand.

PSALM 31:14 THE MESSAGE

The sweetest part of quieting your soul can be awakening our senses to see and hear things we don't normally notice. Whether our home is surrounded by mountains, farmland, rolling hills, a small town, or a big city, there are lots of sights and sounds we grow numb to. They become a backdrop in the busyness of our lives. We lose sight of the fact that little miracles are all around us and there are lots of things to be grateful for in our active, alive, constantly changing environment.

A leisurely walk is one of the best ways to appreciate the gifts we speed past day after day. The slow pace gives us a chance to look longer—at flower gardens we never knew had been planted, at neighbor's homes we didn't know were so quaint, at the renovation of an old building we didn't see happening, or at the new trees that were added to the park's landscape. We miss so much when we hurry so much of the time.

It was no different in Jesus' time: "Jesus said, 'Come off by yourselves; let's take a break and get a little rest.' For there was constant coming and going" (Mark 6:30 THE MESSAGE). Rest is a refuge we all need. We need to create breaks in the constant coming and going of our days. We need to sit for a few minutes without doing anything or take a short walk without thinking about what we have to do next. Breaks cause us to be deliberate about shutting down the demands for a while. Even a small amount of time can make a big difference in how we feel and how we handle life.

In every way and for good reason, it's healthy to slow down. When we slow down our pace, our words, and our reactions, there's a good chance love will prevail in every area of our lives.

Dear God,

Help me slow down and take time
to be thankful for the people in my life
and the good things around me. Give me
the patience and wisdom to respond in
love always.

The Perfect Way to a Peaceful Heart

I'm asking God for one thing, only one thing: To live with Him in His house my whole life long. I'll contemplate His beauty; I'll study at His feet. That's the only quiet, secure place in a noisy world, the perfect getaway, far from the buzz of traffic.

PSALM 27:4–5 THE MESSAGE

We can feel our insides getting tense and our emotions escalating. We hold our tongues and swallow our words, but the stress has nowhere to go. After too many days spent too far away from the quiet, secure place of God's presence, the weariness builds up and we become worn down. We need the peace of God more than ever, and time with Him is the perfect getaway and the perfect way to a peaceful heart.

Most days, the things we spend our time doing are decided for us. Between work and family, there's little left over. We tend to go way beyond the point of weariness before realizing we're in major need of some quiet time.

But it's so good for everyone in our lives if we get into the habit of pursuing and planning time to restore our peace. God is our source of peace, but the way we each choose to spend time with Him is different.

While some of us might put on our running shoes and head out the door, others might take a drive and turn up the worship music. We might tune our spirits in to God's presence and peace by simply sitting quietly on the porch, walking the dog, or staring at the stars. We're uniquely created, so we're uniquely refreshed. God's peace is prevalent in the places we feel most calm, quieted, and reflective.

The more regularly we reset our souls to the peace God gives, the more ready we are to face the tests that come throughout the day. Preparing our hearts and minds with peace can protect us from the worry and stress trying to steal it. It's one of the best ways to bring out the best in us—which is the light of God's unconditional love.

Dear God,

Fill my heart with peace and let me enjoy the quiet strength of Your constant love. Remind me every day how much I need You.

Peace in Any Season

Day and night alike belong to You; You made the starlight and the sun. All nature is within Your hands; You make the summer and the winter too.

PSALM 74:16–17 TLB

Some of the seasons we go through in life are more challenging to our peace than others. During the long "winters" it can seem like God is silent and the answers we're waiting for are frozen in time. It's harder to find our joy in the darkness, even though we know our strength is bound to it. We want to see the snow peaks melt and the mountains move.

C. S. Lewis wisely wrote, "God's presence is not the same as the feeling of God's presence and He may be doing most for us when we think He is doing least".* Our confidence, hope, and peace in the long, difficult seasons of our journey are rooted in *trust*. God doesn't leave us for a moment, even when it feels like He's distant. God uses every single day of our life to prepare us for what's ahead.

Through any season, struggle, or circumstance, the foundation of trusting God is knowing we're *loved* by God—completely, unconditionally, *irrevocably* loved. We can't run from it, and nothing can change it. He loves us with a love that He'll never retract or reconsider. And love *always* does what is best. It's at work in our lives right now, no matter what we see or how we feel.

Today's peace is brought to us by God's love and the faith we have in it! In a world filled with uncertainty and darkness, we can be the light that brings the hope. We know God's love is here, actively working in our lives and seeking a place in *every* heart. The seasons, all of nature, and *every moment of our lives* are in God's hands—wrapped in the most powerful, purposeful love in the universe.

Dear God,

Even in the tough seasons of my life, I trust You completely. Give me peace in Your presence and the love that's shaping every outcome.

*(*The Collected Letters of C. S. Lewis, Volume 3: Narnia, Cambridge and Joy 1950–1963*).

The Significant Habit of Faith

[Jesus said,] "For if you had faith even as small as a tiny mustard seed, you could say to this mountain, 'Move!' and it would go far away. Nothing would be impossible."

MATTHEW 17:20 TLB

Nothing is impossible with God. There isn't a single mountain in our life, Everest or otherwise, that can stand against *seed-sized* faith and the power of God. Tranquillity, prayer, and the tests and trials we go through can build that kind of mountain-shifting faith in us.

Trials grow our patience, and patience has a good work to do in all of us. Expectations become stumbling blocks to our faith when we don't have the patience to *trust* God. We pray and believe, then decide what the answers should be and when they'll come. Trusting God with our whole heart means waiting patiently for the mountain to move—in His perfect time and in the best way.

Prayer fortifies our faith and discourages the desire to control situations we need to surrender to God. Communication and trust are foundations of every relationship, most importantly the one we have with our heavenly Father. Distractions keep us from getting close, hearing clearly, or growing strong spiritually. The only thing God will *ever* speak to us is truth. The more grounded we are in truth, the less wobbly we are in life!

Consistently making time for God is better than feeling pressured to plan a certain amount of time at a precise time every day. Our days change, our schedules vary, and our energy fluctuates. It isn't hard to determine when we need a few minutes to shore up our faith. *When we need it is when we should take it.* Making a habit of keeping it simple is the best way to keep it a priority. Step outside. Close the door. Make a cup of tea. Close your eyes and stretch. Walk around the building, the yard, or the block. Make faith building a simple, *significant* habit. God will meet you there with grace to sustain you, truth to strengthen you, and love to lift you.

Dear God,

I need time with You to be strong, patient, courageous, and trusting. Your words fill me with faith and give me confidence to face whatever the day holds.

Peace in a Power Nap

Great is the Lord, who delights in blessing His servant with peace!

PSALM 35:27 NLT

Sometimes we just need a nap! "Peace in a power nap" would be a great slogan to incorporate into our lives. In a short bit of time, we come away feeling revived, rested, and more peaceful. When we measure the goodness or success of our days by how many to-dos we cross off the list, too often we deny ourselves the simplest good thing in life—*rest*.

We don't have to go through traumatic things to become spiritually and emotionally drained. It can often be the countless, little things we encounter and work through day after day that wear us down. The stress pushes us to an inevitable breaking point, and without warning our peaceful, loving, long-suffering self goes right out the window. That's when we, and everyone around us, wish the nap we needed would've happened.

Sometimes it's impossible to rest *right* when we need to. Demands derail our downtime and the race continues. We push through and keep plugging away. But if we sit still or power nap when we *do* get the chance, we find that a little rest goes a long way when it comes to our well-being.

Stress is one of the worst things for our physical health. That's why God delights in blessing us with peace. He knows it's absolutely necessary in order for our bodies to stay healthy and our spirits to stay strong. Rest and relaxation are perfect pathways to peace. Peace and quiet allow us to enjoy communion with God. Every aspect of peacefulness is healing.

Is there a way to slow things down today—even for a little while? There's always something we *can* be doing, but if we pare down our schedule to what we *have* to do, maybe some rest is doable. The overall benefits outweigh the satisfaction of getting more done. And at the end of the day, feeling better is the far greater blessing.

Dear God,

You're happy when I'm peaceful! Thank You for the blessing of Your peace and for giving me the wisdom to rest when I need to for my physical and spiritual strength.

Revealed in Splendor

There is peace with God through Jesus . . . who is Lord of all creation.

ACTS 10:36 TLB

Nature heightens and deepens our desire to worship. God created the mountain and the stream, the ocean and the sky, the flower and the forest. Because He is the Creator, we see God's design and handiwork in *everything*. The earth holds endless, breathtaking beauty. It would take more than a lifetime to see it all, and it's beyond our human capacity to take it all in. It mirrors the love of God—endless, beautiful, breathtaking, and impossible to fathom.

Maybe you've heard the saying "You should sit in nature for twenty minutes a day . . . unless you're busy, then you should sit for an hour." The healing of our souls that happens when we're surrounded by the handiwork of God is invaluable. God created the earth with us in mind, to fill us with joy, reverence, peace, and praise.

Gratefulness is the heart's response to the endless miracles we see in nature. Who God is reveals itself in splendor. When we see the mountains, we see His majesty. When we see the ocean, we see His might. When we see the trees, we see His strength. When we see the sunrise, we see His faithfulness. When we see the sunset, we see His goodness. When we see the first blooms of spring, we see His kindness. When we see the ladybug, we see His tenderness.

Every living thing matters to God, and we matter most. The life of Jesus revealed the truth of our value. It's as infinite as the universe. When the pressures of this world start to make us forget the value of our lives and the power of our purpose, it's time to restore our peace.

The sun came up this morning and splashed glory across the eastern sky. It's a new day to *know* that our priceless life is in the majestic, mighty, strong, faithful, good, kind, and tender hands of God. Try to get outdoors for some peacefulness and praise—it'll do wonders for your soul.

Dear God,

Peace is a gift You give through the glory of Your creation. I'm thankful for it every day.

An Uncomplicated Life

There is no time to waste, so don't complicate your lives unnecessarily. Keep it simple.

I CORINTHIANS 7:29 THE MESSAGE

When we're alone, it's an opportunity to focus on all the things we're thankful for. Time slows down. Stress falls away. Gratefulness is stirred. Memories bring smiles. Peace settles in. But it's a good chance to practice the art of *clearing* our thoughts too. It's something we rarely do in our fast-paced lives.

Quieting our minds brings our full attention and all our senses into the moment. We notice the things around us: the flowers that miraculously bloomed overnight, the books on the shelf we love but forgot we had, how brilliantly blue the summer sky is, how good the coffee tastes, or how relaxed the sound of a rain shower makes us feel. Being present and observant gives our minds the break they need and invites us to experience the simple joys of life on a soul-refreshing level.

There's nothing difficult about the way God wants us to live. Two things truly matter: loving God and loving others. The expectations of the world, and some we put on ourselves, can make us feel like there's one more goal to reach or a few less pounds and a few more likes needed to gain acceptance. It's not the external image but the internal transformation that ushers us into a fulfilling, meaningful, joyful life.

God loves us just the way we are, and He asks us to love others just the way He does—*unconditionally.* Solitude encourages simplicity, and the silence that often comes with it encourages us to become better listeners. God is always teaching us how to live lives of love. Every time we share love, shower kindness, show compassion, or shine the light of God's joy, we simplify the true gifts of life and the beautiful ways of God.

Dear God,

Make me a vessel of Your goodness.
Inspire me to keep it simple and
straightforward by loving others with a
pure heart and without pause.

In Everything You Do

Trust the Lord completely; don't ever trust yourself. In everything you do, put God first, and He will direct you and crown your efforts with success.

PROVERBS 3:5–6 TLB

Putting God first in everything means we can't leave Him out of *anything* today! Trusting Him completely starts from the time we pour our coffee in the morning to the time we crawl into bed at night. Nothing in our day is insignificant. He cares about every little thing in our lives. It's hard to imagine that the One who holds the earth in the palm of His hand loves us with that kind of fervor, but He does.

"Pray without ceasing" (I Thessalonians 5:17 ESV) goes hand in hand with the proverb "Trust the Lord completely; don't ever trust yourself." It's easy to charge into our day without asking God to help us through it every step of the way. Because so many things are routine for us, we often go through the motions and trust we can handle it. We can, but it might not always be in the best way. For God's wisdom, love, and patience to govern our words and actions, we must *want* His involvement—and we need to *welcome* it through prayer.

God knows what's coming every moment of every day. We're never alone in any storm or crisis, but being prayerfully prepared is the wisest way to stay spiritually strengthened. Prayer is also the best way to sustain peace over panic and faith over fear. When the test comes and the waves start to crash, we can be the one napping in the back of the boat rather than the one doubting God's faithful, loving control of the situation (Mark 4:35–41).

Even when things happen in our lives and we have more questions than answers, we can trust the Lord completely. It's a hard-fought place to get to, but it's the place where peace prevails. Trusting God's direction when the winds are strong and the wait is long will lead us to a good place, *always*—because love won't take us to any other destination.

Dear God,

I want to strengthen my trust in You. Give me wisdom to get out of the way and let You be everything at all times. Thank You for the peace that comes with it.

The One who carved mountains and separated oceans is waiting for us to simply ask for the help we need, then to trust Him with the wisest, best, and most loving response.

"He will give His people strength. He will bless them with peace."

Psalm 29:11 TLB

God's Open Invitation

I will praise You, for I am fearfully and wonderfully made; marvelous are Your works, and that my soul knows very well.

PSALM 139:14 NKJV

Prayer relieves our stress and revives our purpose. It's genuine "God and me" time. It's a chance for us to get clear about where we are in our lives and where we're going, and to listen for some quiet instruction on how to get there. Ideas arise while honest, thoughtful communication takes place without distraction or interruption. It's our time to get raw and real with God and to come away feeling calmed and loved.

God knows us better than anyone else does and loves us better than anyone else can. We need to be reminded of that as often as possible. While we see Him in people, in creation, and in the miracles around us, it's powerful to just sit and *be* in His presence. There's a fullness of joy there that isn't found anywhere else.

If we intertwine prayer with something we love—a nature walk, music that inspires us, a bike ride, gardening, writing, or painting—we experience God's presence even more deeply. What we love has everything to do with the One who knit every part of our being together with thought and intention. It's never good to get forgetful of our unique qualities and the gifts we're given. God has given them to us, and He is glorified through them.

Get away and be quietly held in God's love today. Do what you love for a little while and listen to the still, small voice inside you. It will encourage your gifts, give you direction, and remind you that you're priceless. Peace will refresh you and joy will reenergize you. All the good stuff is in the presence of God, where all the world's stuff fades away. It's a life-giving trade-off—and a soul-soothing, spirit-lifting open invitation from God every single day.

Dear God,

You've given me gifts for Your glory and a deep desire to use them. Renew in me the vision You have for my life and give me the courage to pursue it.

Every Step of the Journey

GOD doesn't come and go. GOD *lasts*. He's Creator of all you can see or imagine. He doesn't get tired out, doesn't pause to catch His breath. And He knows *everything*, inside and out. He energizes those who get tired.

ISAIAH 40:27–29 THE MESSAGE

Some weeks weary us. According-to-plan is rolled over by unpredictable events, news we weren't prepared to hear, and interruptions that put us further behind. By Friday we're tired from body to soul. Contrary to what we want to do when we've fallen behind on our lists, which is to hurry up and work harder, what we really need to do is rest and wait. We need to rest our tired bodies and wait for God to energize our souls.

Our energy doesn't increase by penning a line through a list item. We feel a sense of relief, but we forego the rest we need. God knows us inside and out, and He knows the ins and outs of every situation along life's journey. We can make our plans, but we have to be flexible enough to let

Him direct our steps. We can't see the whole picture. We can't see what's coming or how everything will turn out. We trust God, wait, and step forward in *peace*. If questions or confusion remain, standing still and waiting longer is always the answer.

God's stop signs aren't for testing patience as much as they are for building trust. The more trusting we are, the more peaceful we'll be no matter how much stopping and waiting is required. All the pauses, stops, delays, redirects, and turnarounds we experience are initiated by God's perfect love. Each one keeps our feet on the path of our purpose. Many help us avoid slipping, falling, or failing.

God takes *every step* of our life's journey alongside us, regardless of the terrain changes. The mountains may be steep, the valleys wide, and the deserts seemingly endless, but God isn't going *anywhere*. His love for us has an eternal hold.

Dear God,

When life has me feeling weary and tired, lead my heart to You. Give me rest, recovery, and renewed energy by the power of Your love.

Natural Antidepressant

Your faithfulness extends to every generation, like the earth You created; it endures by Your decree, for everything serves Your plans.

PSALM 119:90–91 TLB

The mountains make us feel small in a good way. It's not a way that makes us feel insignificant but a way that makes us feel humbled by the magnificent God of the universe. His breathtaking beauty goes beyond words. He's at once a place of strength and tranquility. He inspires our deepest reverence and our highest praise. The mountains He sculpted are one of earth's most healing places.

It's been said that being outdoors is a *natural* antidepressant. God's power is evident in every blade of grass and every snowy peak. It is seen in the mighty waves of the ocean and the fragile wings of a butterfly. By His miraculous design, negative ions are *abundant* in nature, especially near waterfalls, at the beach, and in the vastness of the mountains and forests. Negative ions in the air have incredible benefits. They increase the flow of oxygen to the brain, which boosts our energy and helps to balance serotonin levels, making us feel calm and happy.

God is *so* good. He infused healing properties into nature and filled it with beauty, awe, and wonder as a bonus. Our souls can be soothed, satisfied, and strengthened when we're outdoors. It can't be overstated. Creation is ours to appreciate and enjoy. It's proof of God through and through—His divine attributes and eternal power are evident in everything we see. It's hard to imagine surviving the demands of this world without being able to get away from them when we need to.

God's plan for us isn't to race through life without taking time to truly savor the love He put in His design. Every opportunity you have, immerse yourself in God's love and let it fill you with soothing gratefulness. The heavens, the earth, and our *lives* are beautiful reminders of God's caring and calming character. He's going to give you glimpses of His eternal love and faithfulness today—you need only to look for them.

Dear God,

I'm grateful for all You've created to express Your love, care, and the beauty of Your heart. Calm my heart today so I can more fully trust Your plan.

Let Perfect Love Shine Through

May the Lord bless and protect you; may the Lord's face radiate with joy because of you; may He be gracious to you, show you His favor, and give you His peace.

NUMBERS 6:24–26 TLB

When we live a life of kindness, gentleness, compassion, and love, we ignite God's love on earth. *Nothing matters more.* The Lord's face radiates with joy when we honor Him with our lives through the things we do, the people we love, the gifts we engage, and the words we speak. Regardless of how the world measures our worth, being God's light in this world is *true* success. Love lights eternity, and nothing will outlast it.

God's favor is on a life that loves well. And love *magnifies* grace. It's for everyone, at all times, and in any circumstance. Every person God brings into our lives or across our paths should feel loved and showered with grace. Oswald Chambers wrote in *My Utmost for His Highest*, "The knowledge that God has loved me beyond all limits will compel me to go into the world to love others in the same way." *

There are so many temptations our purpose can get tangled up in. Doubt is a big one. We wonder if we're doing enough or if what we're doing has any value. You are and it does! God makes it simple, but we complicate and overthink it. Love can be expressed in a million ways, and the most beautiful part is that the *smallest* gesture can be the difference that changes a life. We all matter, our greatest purpose is love, and every day when the sun comes up God is saying, "Here's the gift of another day to just *love* people."

May the Lord bless and protect you today with the perfect love that shines through your life. May His face be radiantly happy because your life is a reflection of Him. May He be gracious to you and show you favor in everything you do to share His love. May He give you peace in knowing you're *priceless* to Him and nothing can *ever* diminish your value.

Dear God,

There's peace in the purpose You have
for my life, to love You and to love others.
Today, remind me it's that simple and
give me grace to do it well.

* Oswald Chambers, *My Utmost for His Highest* (Uhrichsville, OH: Barbour Books, 1963).

Ordinary Moments

You are glorious and more majestic than the everlasting mountains.

PSALM 76:4 NLT

Driving up a mountain allows us to experience one of the most beautiful transitions of nature—the landscape changes, lakes are crystal clear, the temperature cools, and the sky is a different shade of blue. And then there are the spectacular views. Most of us are overwhelmed trying to take it all in, and we never want to forget how it makes us feel. We want to hold on to the moments that make us feel close to the Creator of everything we see.

Ordinary moments shed light on our extraordinary God too. Because our lives are mostly a collection of everyday things, our hearts can expect to see Him in *all* things. Psalm 71:15 says, "I will tell everyone how good You are, and of Your constant, daily care" (TLB). God's care for us *is* constant. It's there to get us through the tough parts of our day and the anxious parts of our sleepless nights. It's there to celebrate what's special to us and calm the fears that haunt us.

God's true, life-giving words are our constant reminders that He never turns His back or steps away: *I am with you always. I will never leave you. I will never fail you. Don't be afraid. I am here to help you.* Every moment of our lives are blessed with His presence, covered in His grace, and held by His love. Moments are gifts. And not one of them escapes His attention.

We are known and *seen*. Today is in God's constant care. We won't face a challenge without His strength or a fear without His courage. We don't have to go it alone, *ever*—no matter how high we climb, He's as close as this moment and the air we breathe.

Dear God,

I'm secure and sheltered in Your constant love for me. Open my eyes to see You in the moments of my day so that faith and courage always guide me.

Peaceful in the Pages

Mountains rose and valleys sank
to the levels You decreed.

PSALM 104:8 TLB

God called the mountains forth and laid the valleys in place. Both will be part of our life's journey, and God chooses how and when we'll experience each one. Our days are His to direct. He's the author of our stories. Trust is proof that we leave the book in His grip and live fully, thankfully, and joyfully whether we're on the mountaintop or in the deepest, darkest valley.

There's more joy in the valley than we expect, because we discover what it's like to lean on God like never before. When it's dark, when we can't see the next step or the way out, the pain pulls us closer to Him. We cry, we get angry, we get *real*. The vulnerability is one of grief's greatest gifts, and God knows it. His heart meets us there.

And just when we think it's too difficult—too much for too long—the dark gives way to light. *The peace comes, the joy surfaces, the hope emerges, the heart rests.* These are the fruits of letting God have control. His choices are our best pathway through. Trust and hope are our mountain guides for the climb—because it's coming. We'll feel the sun on our faces and see the blue sky again.

When we go from the valley to the peak, our faith will have found a deeper place to take root. It'll be hard to pull us away from trusting God farther ahead on our journey, no matter what we walk through . . . no matter how long the wait is . . . no matter how dark the skies. We'll smile with hope and keep going with courage because God will never let go. The One who penned a powerful purpose into our story before we lived a single page put *eternal* love in the ink—and *nothing* can smudge or erase it.

Dear God,

I trust You with every part of my journey and every word of my story. No matter where it takes me, I know Your love is leading. I'm peaceful in Your purpose for me.

Casting It All

His peace will keep your thoughts and your hearts quiet and at rest.

PHILIPPIANS 4:7 TLB

Every moment alone with the Lord woos our minds to a place of peace. We don't think about being alone; we abide in the presence of God and relish the tranquility. It's meditation time we too seldom get unless we get disciplined about it. There's no doubt we desperately need it. The world is deliberate. It pushes fear and peddles worry. It wants us to buy into the idea that we're on our own in this life, while selling us countless programs and products to help us through.

The first lie is that we're on our own. Jesus debunked that a long time ago: "I am with you always, even to the end of the world" (Matthew 28:20 TLB). The second lie is that we have *anything* to fear. "Fear not, for I am with you. Do not be dismayed. I am your God. I will strengthen you; I will help you; I will uphold you with My victorious right hand" (Isaiah 41:10 TLB). God's right hand is the best fear-fighting solution on the planet. Worry is a weight that wants to be coddled and carried, and we have to choose to *cast* it. "Cast all your anxiety on Him because He cares for you" (I Peter 5:7 NIV).

Solitude strengthens our spiritual muscles. The world is quieted and we hear the still, small voice speaking truth, courage, and hope to our soul. The more we listen, the more we let go. We release the stress and lay down the worry. We let go of our fears and exercise our faith. Our hearts learn how to sustain the quiet and rest that only the peace of God can bring.

Today, God is keeping us. His peace is present. His love is the calm, comforting, refuge for our soul. When the noise of the world comes in, we'll choose *truth*—casting everything else on the One who upholds us with His right hand and unfailing Word.

Dear God,

Let Your truth influence my every thought today so my heart is quiet and at rest in Your perfect peace. Help me to cast all my cares upon You.

At the Top of the List

So we fix our eyes not on what is seen, but on what is unseen, since what is seen is temporary, but what is unseen is eternal.

II CORINTHIANS 4:18 NIV

When days are tough, long, and tiring, God gives us more than enough peace to get us through. *More than enough* defines His character and the measure of all His promises. There's no lack in Him, and there's never a lull in His love for us. It's possible to walk through our hard days with peace, patience, and perseverance.

When God says He'll give us peace that passes understanding, it means we can be at peace when it looks *impossible* to do. Circumstances can't discourage it, people can't affect it, headlines can't steal it, and trials can't destroy it. It's an underlying strength bound to the overarching truth that God is in control, no matter *what* we see.

A peaceful life is God's desire for us, because He knows it's *best* for us. We weren't created for a life that moves along on a steady stream of stress. Work is a part of life, and it's a *good* part. But it should never overwhelm or overtake our peace. If it starts to, it's time to reevaluate how much time we're allowing ourselves to refuel.

Being alone, taking a spiritual wellness day, and praying for wisdom on how to relieve the mounting stress we're under are good ways to navigate our lives back to the peace God gives. He'll give us direction on how to rearrange things, what to let go of, and what to make a priority. Peace will *always* be at the top of the list.

Peace of heart and mind comes with trusting God, heart and soul. We can't have peace if we think we can handle *any* area of our life on our own. Jesus overcame everything in this world that threatens our peace—and the win means that *nothing* in this world can take it from us.

Dear God,

I surrender every area of my life to You. Thank You for the unshakable peace I have in You.

Time to Fill Up

The whole point of what we're urging is simply *love* . . . a life open to God.

I TIMOTHY 1:5 THE MESSAGE

Seeking solitude is one of the sweetest pathways to a life that produces good fruit. When we're intentional about being alone, it encourages our heart to open wide and be refreshed and filled up with every good thing God gives. The spirit of God is overflowing with goodness: love, joy, peace, patience, kindness, and gentleness. What fills our heart comes out in our lives.

Jesus said in Matthew 12:34–35, "Whatever is in your heart determines what you say. A good person produces good things from the treasury of a good heart" (NLT). It's God who fills our hearts and our lives with good things. Giving our souls solitary time with Him every day, or as often as we can, produces the kind of fruit that we want in our lives. It's the spiritual fruit that nourishes far more than the physical well-being of those around us.

We won't have anything to give if we don't set aside time for God to fill us up. He's the endless well of love we draw from and the comfort, grace, and kindness we never want to run out of. His patience is beyond any we can extend, and His hope is higher than any we can offer. God has the stuff that has infinite value and eternal impact. His gifts make the difference we can *never* make without Him.

Thankfully, God is not only a good gift giver; He's a generous one. Our hearts can become rivers that overflow with His goodness *continually*. We can use our times of solitude to make sure our hearts stay full, our spirits stay strong, and our lives stay fruitful—and there's truly nothing sweeter than that.

Dear God,

Fill my heart with the gifts of Your Spirit
so my life becomes a gift to others.

The Test of Two Mountains

We have plenty of hard times . . . but no more so than the good times of His healing comfort—we get a full measure of that, too.

II CORINTHIANS 1:5 THE MESSAGE

There are two kinds of mountain experiences in our lives. There are times when we're standing on the mountain, having made it through a difficult climb that made us stronger, wiser, and able to have an even greater capacity for gratefulness and the magnitude of God's grace. We see things clearly from here—the spiritual growth along the way, the faithfulness of God through the hardest part—and many times, we understand why God chose this path for us.

Then there are times when we need the mountain to *move*. The suffering, the trial, or the circumstances in front of us feel impossible to overcome. We'd rather crawl into a cave in the side of the mountain than stand in faith. We don't see how it can move, we don't know when it will, and we don't fully understand why it's there. But God does. He sees how it will move, He knows when it will happen, and in His perfect love and wisdom He understands why the beauty on the other side is worth getting to.

When we need mountains to move, it is good to remember, "He comes alongside us when we go through hard times, and before you know it, He brings us alongside someone else who is going through hard times so that we can be there for that person just as God was there for us" (II Corinthians 1:3–4 THE MESSAGE). The mountains we face and conquer, with the courage and comfort He gives, will sculpt our lives into a beautiful vessel He can use to pour comfort into the lives of others. *Every ounce of suffering we go through has a purpose.*

Wherever we are in our journey, we can be confident that God is loving and leading us every step of the way. We can stay brave, trusting that something bright and beautiful is coming. And we can be deeply grateful that we're chosen vessels in the Potter's hands, being shaped for His goodness and glory.

Dear God,

Make me all I can be for Your light and love. I'm surrendered to the work of Your hands.

When we nurture
our inner peace,
we give our souls
an anchor to hold
us steady in the
chaos of life.

The Gift of Being Known

My constant boast is God. I can never thank You enough!

PSALM 44:8 TLB

Have you ever sat alone and pondered how much God has blessed you, looked around at God's blessings, and just *smiled big*? You can almost feel your heart swell with gratitude. God might be the only one who sees you beaming, but you can be assured He's smiling with you. It blesses Him to see us humble, thankful, and happy.

Thankfulness is encouraged, expressed, and elevated to high priority throughout God's Word. It's important to God and it's imperative for us. Being thankful brings joy. Being thankful builds confidence. Being thankful belies any temptation to think that the good things in our life come from what *we've* done. Just the opposite is true: "Whatever is good and perfect comes to us from God, the Creator of all light, and He shines forever without change or shadow" (James 1:17 TLB).

No one can out-give God. No one can give as wonderfully or as wisely as God. Knowing us best, He knows what we desire, what we love, and what we *need*. He knows what we need before we ask Him, and He knows what we need before we realize we need it. He prepares us for the obstacles ahead by growing our trust and courage. We look back and think, *Wow. God made me brave for* this—*this challenge only He saw coming.*

The best earthly giftgivers are the people in our lives who truly *know* us. Being known is one of love's most beautiful expressions. It's amazing to realize that even our people—our family and friends—are *good gifts from God.* He knew who we needed and why they'd become a part of our journeys.

Every gift He gives is for His glory, and our gift back to Him is keeping our hearts filled with gratitude.

Dear God,

Every day is another day to be thankful and praise You. Your gifts reveal how intimately You know and love me, and my heart is full.

Peacefulness to Prayer

Shape your worries into prayers.

PHILIPPIANS 4:7 THE MESSAGE

Every now and then it's good to turn off the screens. Lights out for our phones, laptops, and televisions invites the quiet into our lives that goes against the norm. And in the calm comes the peace. Feeling physically at peace helps us connect with the inner peace God gives, and that's the peace we can't live without.

Peacefulness often segues into a contemplative, prayerful state of mind, and every part of our being benefits from it. God's promises of courage, comfort, hope, provision, and direction sink in a little deeper and secure us in His love. In silence we're strengthened in ways we don't realize until the noise and the demands of the world come back in. We face things a little more calmly, we handle things a little more bravely, and we endure things a little more patiently.

A bit of quiet goes a long way. Relaxing even briefly can boost our sense of peacefulness and our mindfulness of God's presence. If we seize the opportunity to open a conversation with Him in prayer, a little bit of quiet time becomes a big reason we get through our day in a God-honoring way. Corrie ten Boom wrote, "What wings are to a bird and sails to a ship, is prayer to the soul".*

Prayer lifts us up and lightens our burdens. It keeps us moving forward smoothly and guides us by the Spirit of God. We find that everything goes better when we're prayed up, and if something does go wrong, we're better prepared to deal with it. Our peace of heart and mind has been strengthened in prayer. The patience, kindness, and compassion of God kicks in, and the outcome brings Him glory rather than bringing us guilt for reacting in our emotions.

A screen shutdown would be good today. Opt for peacefulness and prayer. Start making some out-of-the-norm quiet your normal routine. God's going to *love* spending more time together.

Dear God,

Even on days when it's hard to slow down, help me make prayer and peace a priority.

*Corrie ten Boom, *Clippings from My Notebook* (Waterville, ME, Thorndike Press, 1983), 89.

Striking the Balance

Search high and low, scan skies and land,
you'll find nothing and no one quite like God.

PSALM 89:5–6 THE MESSAGE

How often do we find ourselves at the end of the day feeling like there's more to do than we got done? Which means there's even more to do tomorrow. Then there are things we file mentally under *Don't forget to __________ (fill in the blank).* We leave out, forget, or skip over what we *really* need to do.

Balance stands in stark contrast to what our days usually look like. Napping is a lost art, sitting on a porch swing is somewhat historical, and lounging in a hammock is saved for a yearly vacation. We've nearly forgotten how to step away—in any way we can—from the nonstop, clamoring, cluttered world we live in. Where is the balance?

Thank God for the provision of nature. We probably don't have to venture far from our homes to get to a place or a park where there are more trees than people, where the birds can be heard over the traffic, and where green grass stretches out like a carpet for us to picnic on. God is so *good*. He knows what we need to be healthy, whole, and at peace. "Everything God does is right—the trademark on all His works is love" (Psalm 145:17 THE MESSAGE). His love provides the balance our lives need.

Love is the reason we need to break out of our routines. *Regularly*. God saturated creation with love, peace, miracles, and joy. It's a way to see how intricately and intimately He put His heart into His handiwork. It inspires praise, lifts our spirits, and feeds our souls so we can keep the demands of the day in balance. God didn't leave a *single* detail to chance. It shows, and it's *breathtaking*.

Get some quiet time in today. Go outdoors if you can. Look for the love of God everywhere and know that all He created is a living love letter to us, His *crowning* creation. It will bring the perfect balance to a hectic day.

Dear God,

I see Your life and love in nature, and I'm thankful for the way it balances my stress, restores calm, and refreshes my soul.

Peace in Every Way

May the Lord of peace Himself give you peace at all times and in every way.

II THESSALONIANS 3:16 NIV

We will have times in our lives that are sad, sometimes overwhelmingly so. Loss and change are part of life, just as restoration and redemption are. We should never hesitate to ask God to reveal His tender love and comforting presence in personal ways. He might use a surprise visit or a call from a friend or unexpected little miracles in the world around us to let us know He sees us and is acquainted with our grief.

"The LORD is close to the brokenhearted and saves those who are crushed in spirit" (Psalm 34:18 NIV) reminds us of His constant attention. God's compassion toward us *will not* fail. He hears our hearts before we speak and counts our tears before they come. He's here in this moment to give us peace in every way. We can trust Him—with the questions, the sadness, the fear, the pain—and know He'll bear the weight of it and carry us through.

God gives the peace that sustains us during the silent, searching hours. We can't find words and we can't see how light will ever pierce the heartbreaking darkness, but we hold on because we know He's holding on to us. Our hope is in Him alone. The peace that passes understanding will keep the light of that hope going, and in time the flicker will become a flame.

Pay close attention today. God's encouragement, divine nature, loving presence, and endless compassion can be seen everywhere. It's in a spectacular sunrise, a refreshing breeze, a birdsong, and a bloom. It's in the starry sky, the milky moon, the spring rain, and the towering trees. We are *never* without His enveloping love and grace.

"You comprehend my path and my lying down, and are acquainted with all my ways" (Psalm 139:3 NKJV). When we immerse ourselves in the promises of God's peace and presence, we can embrace the courage that carries us through.

Dear God,

You know and love me in ways no one else does or can. Your sustaining peace is with me today, and my hope is in You alone.

Unbreakable Peace

The mountains may depart and the hills disappear, but My kindness shall not leave you. My promise of peace for you will never be broken, says the Lord.

ISAIAH 54:10 TLB

God gives us peace that can't be broken. It's not going to crack when life falls apart, it's not going to break when our hearts do, and it's not going to shatter when our dreams are in a million pieces. The peace of God anchors us while He puts everything together at the perfect time and in the most purposeful way.

It's human to feel a sense of urgency when it comes to seeing our hopes come to fruition. We do everything we can do—trust God, dream big, work hard, and stay committed. But wisdom keeps our hearts and minds peaceful in the process. Our trust grows deeper during the wait, and maybe that's part of God's purpose in it. Only He knows how to prepare our hearts for what's coming. It's bigger than we can imagine!

God loves us too much to take us through anything that doesn't have the most loving outcome. As prolonged and painful as the path can be, God is creating something beautiful *in* us that is bound to eternity. With everything we go through, holding Him closely, trusting Him completely, and surrendering to Him fully has *infinite* value. The true and lasting gifts are the ones our hearts receive.

Being at peace with what God chooses for our lives is the key to having the *best* life. What He gives is what we need, what He allows is what we need to grow stronger, and the place He leads us to is *exactly* where we need to be.

Dear God,

Fill my heart with the peace that can't be broken. Give me a patient, surrendered spirit as You work out what is best for my life according to Your perfect plan and unstoppable love.

A Little Wandering

I stand silently before the Lord, waiting for Him to rescue me.

PSALM 62:1 TLB

Some days it feels like we need a rescue. These are the best days for a hike or a long walk in nature, where the scenery invites us to stand silently and wait. We wait for our thoughts to settle and our hearts to become peaceful. We wait to allow the Spirit of God to surround us with the comfort promised and the strength we need. We wait to hear the quiet, gentle voice within us whisper, "Everything is going to be okay."

No matter what life looks like at present, we can trust we're not alone. Sometimes it takes getting away from everything and everybody to realize how near God is and how aware He is of what we're going through. And it's important to do. Even taking a drive through our favorite areas to absorb the beauty while listening to good music is enough to savor God's closeness to us. He's in the good things. He's the giver of whatever it is that feeds our souls and draws us to Him.

It doesn't take a long time in the daily grind or a lot of reading the latest headlines to realize we aren't getting any peace in this world outside of God. He's our place of refuge and our perfect hideaway. He's the only way through this messy world. He's the solid ground in our sinking circumstances and the rescuing love in our wearied hope. He's here to see us beyond what we see with the *best* promise: "I have made you and I will carry you; I will sustain you and I will rescue you" (Isaiah 46:4 NIV).

When the day begins with a weary heart, do a little wandering. Wander away from the noise. Live and breathe His presence in the good things around you. See His grace in the sunrise and His faithfulness when it sets. See His beauty in a blue sky or His joy in a bird singing from a treetop. He's here, hoping you'll notice and remember that *you are* seen every moment of every day. You're seen, you're known, you're loved, and you're rescued—by the One who will *never* fail you.

Dear God,

Hold me close when I'm weary and open my eyes to the constant, unwavering love surrounding me.

A Place and Purpose

My purpose is to give life in all its fullness.

JOHN 10:10 TLB

It's not going to be a place, a position, or a perfect circumstance that gives us true peace; it's going to come through the overcomer of the world. It's not going to be a world-derived solution that helps us get through our days; it's going to be the supernatural strength of God. And it's not going to be through earthly avenues that we discover our deepest purpose, because it's found in the One who created the earth and everything in it—and that includes us!

Every day is a good day to let the peace of God push out the stress. It's good to daily surrender our worries and meditate on how perfectly God cares for us and how perfectly we're created to follow our hearts' passions. We've been given all we need to do the things in life God has for us to do, to live our lives to the fullest. It's so important to take time to listen to our hearts.

The love of God will lead us. Even when it looks like

our lives have been derailed or overrun by pressures from the world or expectations we put on ourselves. Grace has all the giving room we'll ever need. It reaches us even when we're running in the wrong direction—frustrated by disappointment, fighting against fear, and forgetting the truth. We lose sight of the power and determination of God's love. We can *never* be separated from it.

"God made everything with a place and purpose" (Proverbs 16:4 THE MESSAGE). When we're in a difficult place, even as the result of our choices, God's love is with us to guide our steps gently and faithfully. And the beautiful part is, He'll use everything we go through to help us grow and to reveal the deeply devoted, absolute, and *immovable* nature of His love.

Dear God,

The desires of my heart begin with You.
The path of my purpose is in Your hands.
Give me wisdom to hear You and faith to follow You every day.

In the Palm of His Hand

I will not forget you. See, I have inscribed you on the palms of My hands.

ISAIAH 49:15–16 NKJV

What does the peace of God do in us when everything around us is *anything* but calm? The roots of our peace go deeper in the trust we have in Him. We dig down to hold on, we believe He hasn't let go, and we know His grace will get us through. When things seem to hurtle out of control, God is at work, His faithfulness won't fail, and nothing has escaped the palm of His hand.

Our peace has an insurance policy, procured by Jesus: "My Father, who has given them to Me, is greater than all; no one can snatch them out of My Father's hand" (John 10:29 NIV). There's no greater promise securing our rest. God's got us! He's holding us when things don't go the way we planned; He's holding us when it looks like darkness is winning and light is fading; and He's holding us when all else is falling apart, failing, or testing every fiber of our being.

There isn't anything happening on earth or in our lives that God isn't aware of. It's easy to question it sometimes, but there's never going to be a different answer: "The earth belongs to God! Everything in all the world is His!" (Psalm 24:1 TLB). Until we see with our eyes the *good* God will bring from seemingly impossible and unredeemable events, trust is our lifeline. Faith is our focus. And peace is our security in the storm.

It's possible to have peace today, no matter what we're going through or what's going on around us. The peace of God doesn't fluctuate. God is faithful even when we're fickle. And we can be. We're human, and our emotions want their way. But faith doesn't give us the freedom to follow our feelings. We can't let our trust be temperamental. God is *never* going to fail us. His love is all-consuming, His truth is all-powerful, and His peace is *all* ours at *all* times.

Dear God,

I praise You for giving me peace in every circumstance. Nothing can shake my trust in You. Thank You for keeping me in the palm of Your hand.

What Matters Most

Don't you know by now that the everlasting God, the Creator of the farthest parts of the earth, never grows faint or weary?

ISAIAH 40:28 TLB

There's a sense of time standing still in the mountains. Silence settles in, and the rock faces stand formidable against the fragility of our small frames. It's breathtaking, grounding, and humbling. It helps us understand more clearly the awesome splendor of God and the amazing truth that He *loves* us with a love that seeps in to *every detail* of our lives.

God's love towers above every mountain on earth and reaches beyond the depth of every ocean. It's a love as unstoppable as the sunrise and as sure as the sunset that follows. We're a tiny part of an *infinite* universe, and our lives are infinitely valued by the One who created us. It's hard to wrap our minds around that kind of love, and it can be even harder to believe it on the days we don't feel lovable at all.

We lose our patience, ride every emotion, ignore God's direction, and forge ahead without seeking His wisdom.

We keep going until we're exhausted or feeling defeated by the inevitable consequences of quick, unguided decisions. And there, in that dismal place, we're still surrounded by God's monumental love. He is graciously ready to pick us up and put us back on our feet.

God is never going to grow weary of us. He's not going to get tired of loving us or caring about everything in our lives. We might think we don't need to bother Him with every little thing that comes up, but He'd love for us to get into the habit of doing it—because it *all* matters to Him. What matters most to Him is the condition of our heart, the place within us He wants securely *trusting in Him*. Because He never grows faint or weary, we can stand in faith knowing He'll always give us the strength and courage we need, from a heart of boundless love.

Dear God,

I'm in awe of Your absolute love for me and humbled by Your attention to the smallest detail of my life. My heart trusts in You alone.

In peace
I will lie down
and sleep, for
You alone,
O LORD, will
keep me safe.

PSALM 4:8 NLT

Peace in His Presence

Pay all your debts except the debt of love for others—never finish paying that! For if you love them, you will be obeying all of God's laws.

ROMANS 13:8 TLB

We never outgrow the importance of *resting* when we need to. It helps us behave better. We're more likely to love instead of lose our patience, respond softly instead of stressfully, and to treat people the way our heavenly Father has taught us to. "Here is a simple, rule-of-thumb guide for behavior: Ask yourself what you want people to do for you, then grab the initiative and do it for them. Add up God's Law . . . and this is what you get" (Matthew 7:12 THE MESSAGE).

Taking advantage of even the smallest space of rest we can squeeze into our day can bring big changes in our attitude and overall health. It doesn't matter if we spend the time reflecting, praying, reading, writing, gardening, or napping—whatever resets our soul to peacefulness is what we should do. It doesn't have to be the same thing every day, and it probably won't be.

When we walk in peace and love with the people in our lives, it makes every part of our lives better. Our hearts rest, as opposed to being bogged down with regret. When we've taken time to prioritize the quiet time we need to let God renew our strength and refresh our spirits, everybody wins. Love is a lot of things, and it's also *not* a lot things—proud, rude, demanding, or irritable.

We can avoid sliding into our emotional, non-loving behaviors if we give God the chance to love on us through *real rest*. Jesus encouraged us to come to Him to find the rest we need—and the encouragement, light, joy, and love we find in His presence is all we need to be the best we can be. Loving people best is how our lives are *truly* blessed—with peace, joy, and every good thing love *is*.

Dear God,

Give me a heart that loves as You do. Teach me how to rest in Your presence so that I can be a clearer reflection of Your love to the people in my life.

All of Nature Rejoice

Let the vast seas roar, let the countryside and everything in it rejoice!

I CHRONICLES 16:32 TLB

It's impossible to escape the opportunity for worship in nature. From the serenity of a pastoral landscape to the beauty of a city park sprinkled with duck ponds and flowerbeds, from the inspiration of a walk on the beach to the breathtaking views on a mountain climb—God's presence seems a tangible, wonderful part. It's God's way of gifting us the contentment our souls crave.

Nature provides the pressure release our minds and bodies need. The natural world is a sweet reminder to rejoice in His all-encompassing love. God made it that simple. As lovely as our homes are, as therapeutic as shopping can be, nothing makes our souls sing like the crashing waves of an ocean or the field full of wildflowers.

"If God hadn't been there for me, I never would have made it. The minute I said, 'I'm slipping, I'm falling,' Your love, GOD, took hold and held me fast. When I was upset and beside myself, You calmed me down and cheered me up" (Psalm 94:16–19 THE MESSAGE). We don't slip. We don't fall. We rejoice in God's calming force. He's our joy source. He's present, peaceful, and powerful. He wants to help us through life, and He wants us to have a lives filled with every good thing He gives.

When the day has you feeling like you're slipping away from a joyful place, step outside and take a deep breath. Draw on God's strength while seeing Him in every created thing. His love is here to calm us down and cheer us up. Join all of nature in the constant chorus of praise, while His perfect peace fills your heart and mind.

Dear God,

I love seeing You in all of nature and knowing You're present through the peace it restores in me.

Standing Prepared

Be prepared. You're up against far more than you can handle on your own. Take all the help you can get, every weapon God has issued, so that when it's all over but the shouting you'll still be on your feet. Truth, righteousness, peace, faith, and salvation are more than words. Learn how to apply them. You'll need them throughout your life.

EPHESIANS 6:13–15 THE MESSAGE

The first rule of mountain climbing is to be prepared for what you'll encounter on the way up. There will be expected challenges like changing weather patterns, physical adjustments to higher altitudes, and increasing strength demands on your body. There might be some unexpected things, too, like rock falls, equipment failures, or avalanches. It's not an easy venture, but being fully prepared increases the chance of standing on the summit or getting to the set goal.

Living the life God wants for us—one that's abundantly blessed, fulfilling, and overcoming—has a lot to do with preparation. The "equipment" we're encouraged to have with us at all times is a spiritual collection that includes truth, peace, and trust. God knows we can't do this alone.

The journey is riddled with things we don't see coming, things only He can strengthen us for through His Word and the power of prayer.

We all experience heartbreaking loss, changing circumstances, and disappointments that feel devastating. God is undeniably *close* to us, often carrying us during those times. But we can determine to be as prepared as we possibly can with *truth*. "Whatever I have, wherever I am, I can make it through anything in the One who makes me who I am" (Philippians 4:13 THE MESSAGE).

With God's strength, we can do the unthinkable and the unexpected, and we can respond to the obstacles of life in a way that is *unlike this world*: "Be cheerful no matter what; pray all the time; thank God no matter what happens. This is the way God wants you who belong to Christ Jesus to live" (I Thessalonians 5:18 THE MESSAGE). Being prepared with truth helps us go through life with a peace that passes understanding—and keeps us standing in the midst of it all.

Dear God,

Give me wisdom to prepare for what's ahead on my journey, and fill me with the peace that sustains me through whatever comes.

All the Courage We Need

God's loyal love couldn't have run out,
His merciful love couldn't have dried
up. They're created new every morning.
How great Your faithfulness!

LAMENTATIONS 3:22–23 THE MESSAGE

The sun breaks the horizon to begin a new day. With it comes new mercy and a clean slate for all. The world is slowly waking up from its slumber before reaching its full, fevered pitch. The morning is a special time for quiet time. If we can take advantage of it, it is the best spirit-strengthening exercise, one that will affect our day in a good way from beginning to end.

Life is a series of ups and downs, so many of them falling outside the realm of our control. Sometimes we have more questions than answers, more heartbreak than happiness, and more waiting than we're able to handle with trust and patience. But we keep going when it's harder than we expect because of the strength we receive in our solitude—during those one-on-one conversations with God.

It doesn't have to feel like God is present for us to be certain that He is. He hears every word, sees every tear, and understands every plea. "He listens the split second I call to Him" (Psalm 4:3 THE MESSAGE). He hurts when we do, even though it's almost impossible to imagine that kind of concerned, compassionate, and caring love coming from the One who counts and names trillions of stars. How can He bend down to discern the whispers of our hearts? He can and He *does*.

"He does what's best for those who fear Him—hears them call out, and saves them" (Psalm 145:19 THE MESSAGE). There isn't a *miniscule* space between our need and God's love. Our lives are bound to His and His love is bound to us—and it's a love that gives all the courage we'll need to face today with peace.

Dear God,

Your faithfulness and grace are my constant covering, and I can have perfect peace in the shelter of them.

The Praises of Heaven

Sing, O heavens! Be joyful, O earth! And break out in singing, O mountains! For the Lord has comforted His people.

ISAIAH 49:13 NKJV

Praise is a source of perpetual peace. It's also a powerful pick-me-up. All of nature rejoices in God, and part of His creation is even humming a *constant* chorus. It's been discovered that the stars in the universe perform a celestial concert that never stops. Big stars make low, deep sounds, and small stars have high-pitched "voices." We live beneath a *canopy* of continuous praise—no wonder stargazing inspires awe, humility, and peace within us.

Every day brings different challenges to our trust, our hope, and our peace. We rarely get a day off from the pressures of life. But we can create *pockets of praise* within them.

We can drown our discouragement in gratefulness: "No matter what happens, always be thankful" (I Thessalonians 5:18 TLB); "Think about all you can praise God for and be glad about" (Philippians 4:8 TLB).

We can blanket our fears in truth: "If God is on our side, who can ever be against us?" (Romans 8:31 TLB); "Fear not, for I am with you. Do not be dismayed. I am your God. I will strengthen you; I will help you" (Isaiah 41:10 TLB).

We can wrap our hope in promises: "May the God of hope fill you with all joy and peace in believing, that you may abound in hope by the power of the Holy Spirit" (Romans 15:13 NKJV); "Glory be to God, who by His mighty power at work within us is able to do far more than we would ever dare to ask or even dream of—infinitely beyond our highest prayers, desires, thoughts, or hopes" (Ephesians 3:20 TLB).

Bring the power of praise into your day. Be mindful of the love that filters every single thing in our lives. Nothing happens outside of God's promise: "I am with you." He has us in His hand at *every* moment, and our hearts can join the continuous chorus of creation's praise.

Dear God,

Every time I look up at a star-filled sky,
my heart will join the *constant* chorus of
praise.

Savor Every Second

He gives power to the tired and worn out, and strength to the weak.

ISAIAH 40:29 TLB

Every part of our being gets tired at some point. Some jobs are physical, while others tax us mentally. Some put a strain on both. We *all* need breaks from the cycle of our day-to-day. Not only do breaks refresh us for the return to our routine, but they also reenergize us so that we can be our stronger, more patient selves. The light of God in us can grow dim if we don't recharge. Time away from it all is a good source for getting the boost we need.

The most important reason for resting our hearts, souls, and minds is so we don't get too worn out to do the most important things; "Let's not allow ourselves to get fatigued doing good. At the right time we will harvest a good crop if we don't give up, or quit" (Galatians 6:9 THE MESSAGE). God meets us in the quiet times we set aside for the very purpose of *strengthening* us, *refreshing* us, and *preparing* us. We're here to do good, be a light, and bring

Him glory. It's hard to do that when we feel wiped out from the daily grind.

What will the time you take to let God restore you look like today? Will it be taking a peaceful walk, sitting in your favorite chair with a cup of coffee, or spending time in the yard to notice what's blooming? Whatever it is that invites God in to soothe your soul, do that—and savor every second of it.

Dear God,

Remind me regularly how much I *need* You. Make me mindful of Your desire to refresh me for the good work I'm created to do.

God Revealed

It's wonderful what happens when Christ displaces worry at the center of your life.

PHILIPPIANS 4:7 THE MESSAGE

The way God reveals His character in the created world is often both breathtaking and soothing. We marvel at countless sunsets and take as many photos as possible of them, yet we're drawn to stand, watch, and snap countless more. There's something about the colors, the brevity of the sinking sun when it touches the horizon, and the chance to quietly reflect on another day. God's faithfulness is in it, and we feel thankful.

Seasons reveal the blessings of God's provision, the beauty of change, the miracle of life from death, and His indisputable presence and glory in all the earth. Nature is a gift that displaces the worry and anxiety we battle every day, replacing it with peace and tranquility. That, in turn, allows Christ to become the center of our lives.

Finding ways to rebuild our inner peace and redistribute every worry from our hearts to God's hand is essential to our wellness. He wants to carry our worries. He wants to calm our fears. He wants to create in us hearts that *trust Him completely*. He wants to be our peace, provision, strength, and security—all we have to do is courageously and confidently let Him be our *all in all.*

Dear God,

I know peace is part of Your perfect provision for my life. I'm thankful for the ways it's restored through the gift of Your creation, Your presence, and Your constant love.

Peace without a View

And we know that in all things God works for the good of those who love Him, who have been called according to His purpose.

ROMANS 8:28 NIV

Everything looks different from a higher altitude. The farther we climb, the smaller the world below appears. The view becomes panoramic. We see the outlines of towns, the edges of fields and forests, and the shapes of lakes and rivers. If we could have that kind of perspective when it comes to our lives, we'd be less anxious and it would be easier to trust God with the outcome. But God doesn't give us the far-and-wide lens on what He's doing, even though we'd like Him to most of the time.

Some days it's just plain hard to go forward when we don't understand what God is doing in our lives. From heaven's view, and with the perfect love in His heart, He's laying things out, working everything into place, and creating the most beautiful landscape in our lives—one we can only see unfold a day at a time.

If we could see the meaning in every test, the things He's preparing us for, or the lives we'll affect through the maturing of our faith, we'd be in awe of the view. It would show how God shapes our lives into an intricate pattern that reveals His perfect love, endless grace, and eternal goodness. But the depth of our love and trust couldn't and wouldn't increase if we were given a bird's-eye view along the way.

God is the most loving Father, whose purpose prevails in the most loving way. We can trust Him completely. When the path ahead is dark and we're weary, His peace will guide us one step at a time. We can know that from where He sits, each of our lives is becoming a *breathtaking* view—edged with grace, shaped by love, and outlined with the beauty of becoming the reflection of Him.

Dear God,

I trust my day, my life, and my purpose to the loving design of Your heart and hands. Give me peace as I surrender all to You.

The Peace that Remains

Can any one of you by worrying add a single hour to your life?

MATTHEW 6:27 NIV

Abiding peace. Peace that stays with us, holds us steady, calms our emotions, and drums with every heartbeat—*everything is going to be okay.* That's the peace we get when we trust God. It's the peace that remains when it looks like the world is in ruins and darkness is winning. "His life is the light that shines through the darkness—and the darkness can never extinguish it" (John 1:5 TLB).

In the toughest times, when we don't understand the reasoning or the plan and we're battle worn, are times when the peace of God comes in like a flood. There are countless stories of people who've been in extremely difficult situations and felt an indescribable peace come over them. When our hearts cry out, God answers. He can be trusted when we're tried beyond our limits. He's the strength of our hearts and our hope forever.

"Be strong. Take courage. Don't be intimidated . . . because GOD, your God, is striding ahead of you. He's right there with you. He won't let you down; He won't leave you" (Deuteronomy 31:6 THE MESSAGE). God has gone ahead of us and sees us on the other side of the storm. He doesn't leave us alone in the struggle and fear. He's right here, right now. He's here for us to lean on, ready to lift us up when we need Him to. Love is stronger than anything we face. It's kind, caring, faithful, and *trustworthy*. Everything love is, God brings to the fight—and *nothing* can overcome it.

When worry tries to make its way into your day, use truth to push it out! "He alone is my refuge, my place of safety; He is my God, and I am trusting Him" (Psalm 91:2 TLB); "I am holding you by your right hand—I, the Lord your God—and I say to you, Don't be afraid; I am here to help you" (Isaiah 41:13 TLB). Worry won't add a single hour to our lives, but the peace of God will give our hearts all the strength they need for today.

Dear God,

Fill my heart with courage and peace.
Help me stand on truth and hope in
You alone.

Hitting the Brakes

God, order a peaceful and whole life for us because everything we've done, You've done for us.

ISAIAH 26:11–12 THE MESSAGE

On some days, breathing is enough. You don't have to accomplish a single thing to prove your worth. You can tuck the lists away, turn off the phone, and feel free to do whatever makes you happy, inspires peace, and settles your soul. Listen for sounds you never stop to hear, look for wonders you never have time to see, and breathe in all the fresh air you need. God, who created all these things, is here, reminding us that it is in Him that we find our *infinite* worth.

God doesn't forget how much we need Him, even when we race through our days. The weeks flow together in routine, nonstop motion, and *we do the forgetting*. He loves us patiently, provides for us faithfully, and paves our paths with inexhaustible grace. His kindness toward us doesn't change because *He* doesn't change, and His love for us is greater than we'll ever be able to comprehend.

At some point in our hurried, hectic pace, our souls know it's time to hit the brakes. When that happens, we have to rest and rediscover that all the going and doing doesn't define us *or* our worth. God's definition is the one that holds true and truly matters. He tells us, "You are precious to Me and honored, and I love you" (Isaiah 43:4 TLB). You're wonderfully, marvelously made by the One who unconditionally and undeniably *loves* you! Nothing can separate you from God's love, and nothing in this world can diminish your worth to Him.

Take a day every once in a while to simply enjoy being loved to that magnitude. And when you do, love God back through gratefulness and praise, and peacefully pay attention to the goodness He has placed *all around* us.

Dear God,

I'm humbled by Your unchanging love, undeserved grace, and overwhelming goodness in my life. Remind me to rest in it more often.

[God] has infinite attention to spare for each one of us. He doesn't have to deal with us in the mass. You are as much alone with Him as if you were the only being He had ever created.

C. S. LEWIS

Growing Peace through Patience

We are able to hold our heads high no matter what happens and know that all is well, for we know how dearly God loves us.

ROMANS 5:5 TLB

Getting to the place where we're at peace in any storm or circumstance we go through in life takes time. Going from trial to trust is on repeat throughout each of our journeys, and we're continually learning how dependable God is. His faithfulness is absolute and unwavering. "Count it all joy when you fall into various trials, knowing that the testing of your faith produces patience. But let patience have its perfect work, that you may be perfect and complete, lacking nothing" (James 1:2–4 NKJV).

With the patience produced by every test of our faith, our ability to trust and be at peace grows too. It's difficult to put our trials in the joy column of life. But when we get through them, we see how we've drawn closer to God and how the roots of our faith have gone deeper. We understand the purpose God had for it and the beauty He brought out of it.

We never want to get to a stagnant place in our relationship with God. We should have a consistent, courageous desire to know Him more intimately, trust Him more fully, and love Him more joyfully. Every area of our lives gets better when we know God better. The love He has for us is a balm for our wounds, a barrier against our fears, and a beacon in our darkness. It holds hope high when we're at our lowest.

We can be brave today and say, "All is well because I know how much God loves me." We can be confident no matter what happens because God's love is stronger than the waves and wind in any storm. We can rest because calm is coming, patience is working, and peace is growing deeper still.

Dear God,

Help me hold my head high today in the midst of any struggle or storm that comes. You're working all things together with Your loving heart, for my growth and the beauty it brings.

A Mountain of Purpose

He lets me rest in the meadow grass and leads me beside the quiet streams. He gives me new strength.

PSALM 23:2–3 TLB

Every mountain we come to in our lives has a purpose. It's there to challenge our faith and make us stronger. When our trust gets stronger, our peace goes deeper. Our part in the purpose of any trial is to *trust God*. We don't have to strive, struggle, or search for all the answers—we only have to let Him lead us. He gives us rest and peace in all things, at all times, even when our problems look like mountains we can't possibly conquer.

We won't scale or move *any* mountain on our own, and we don't have to try. The battle is never ours to fight, the mountain is never ours to move, and the storm is never ours to calm. We simply have to trust the One who overcame the world. Jesus is the conquering warrior, the mountain mover, and the master of the wind. The grace He won is why we can go through this world with peace of heart and mind.

So how do we hold on to the peace of God? We fill our hearts and minds with truth. *Every day.* This world will give us a thousand things to think about, watch, and worry over; it's up to us to decide whether we'll allow those things to take over our thoughts. It's a constant bombardment. We pick up our phones to scroll, and before we know it, we've spent an hour of priceless time in our day doing something that does nothing to nurture our peace.

Quiet time, nature, truth, and trust are some of the best ways to ground ourselves in the peace of God. Just the thought of sitting beside a quiet stream usually puts our minds in a good place. Psalm 23 reminds us that God gives us new strength in peacefulness and rest, and we can all use some of that to get through our days, even when there *isn't* a mountain in front of us.

Dear God,

Thank You for truth, grace, peace, and Jesus. There's nothing we can't overcome together.

Spiritual Strengthening

God, I'm not trying to rule the roost, I don't want to be king of the mountain. . . . I've kept my feet on the ground, I've cultivated a quiet heart.

PSALM 131:1–2 THE MESSAGE

Solitude has more perks than just getting away from things that are trying our nerves or draining our patience. It's far more beneficial than a break from the mayhem. Naturally, our bodies feel an immediate sense of relief, our breathing slows, and the tension starts to release its hold when we disengage. These are the obvious good things. But the *best* good thing about calming down physically and setting our hearts and minds on God and His Word is that we open up spiritually.

"May the God of hope fill you with all joy and peace as you trust in Him, so that you may overflow with hope by the power of the Holy Spirit" (Romans 15:13 NIV). That's a lot of good stuff coming through! Joy, *peace*, and overflowing hope are the kind of things we want to have in us at all times. But life brings the peace busters—job pressures, unexpected news, and a world growing darker. When things that are out of our control start to mount, our reactions aren't always in keeping with the Spirit-led response we'd like to have.

Solitude gives us a restart in our relationship with God. In that quiet place we calm down and pray up. God meets us in the silence, strengthening our spirits. There isn't a more powerful pick-me-up. So many things in our life, no matter how pressing they seem, can *wait* while we recharge. Simple things satisfy us on a deeper level than we realize. Things like going into the kitchen to make something comforting, taking a quick nap, getting outside for a few minutes, going for a bike ride, or just sitting quietly.

Jesus knew how necessary it was to spend time with God, and we want to follow His example. We can't stay physically well if we don't stay spiritually strong. Worry is draining and stress is unhealthy. God wants to relieve us of both—it is up to us to turn it all over to Him as *often* as we need to.

Dear God,

I surrender all the big and little things in my life to Your care and control today. Thank You for the strength and hope You give.

Beautiful Simplicity

May God give you more and more mercy, peace, and love.

JUDE 2 NLT

If we had to identify the culprit that most often comes to steal our peace, what would it be? Would it be a work-related issue, the lies of comparison, or our own negative self-talk? It's difficult to stay Spirit-minded in a performance- and image-driven world. The apostle Paul couldn't have known what life would look like now, but he gave us timeless words of wisdom that couldn't be more spot-on: "Don't copy the behavior and customs of this world, but let God transform you into a new person by changing the way you think. Then you will learn to know God's will for you, which is good and pleasing and perfect" (Romans 12:2 NLT).

Peace and contentment are hard-fought these days. We have the constant temptation to compare ourselves to others through a device we carry around *in the palms of our hands*. The scope of comparison goes beyond our immediate circle. We have access to the entire world! We can "follow" the lives of people we've *never* met. Again, the words of truth give perspective: "Everything else is worthless when compared with the priceless gain of knowing Christ Jesus my Lord" (Philippians 3:8 TLB). There is nothing in this world worth more than what we already have in Jesus.

Contentment and peace go hand in hand. If we learn how *beautiful* simplicity is—a life built on love, kindness, and Christ—we gain everything worth having in this world. We also gain the blessing of a truly fulfilling life, lived in the center of God's will. It begins and ends with love, because that's what God *is*. And "godliness with contentment is great gain" (I Timothy 6:6 NIV).

What can we do today to cultivate peace and conquer whatever tries to take it? Start with a thankful heart and a focus on love. Enjoy some quiet time, look for simple joys, and see the goodness in everything you have *right now*.

Dear God,

Your love and grace are all I need, and I'm thankful for the eternal, irreplaceable gifts You've given.

Kindness in the Morning

Let me see Your kindness to me in the morning, for I am trusting You. Show me where to walk, for my prayer is sincere.

PSALM 143:8 TLB

Morning quiet is different from any other quiet time in our day. When the sun comes up, the world feels new and hopeful. Mercy has whitewashed the mistakes of yesterday and given us confidence that God's grace will walk us through today. It's a sweet time in His presence and a great time to enjoy some solitude before the demands of the day are off and running.

"Every morning tell Him, 'Thank You for Your kindness,' and every evening rejoice in all His faithfulness" (Psalm 92:2 TLB). What a perfect bookend habit for our days. It's a reminder that God's kindness and faithfulness are things we can count on completely. God's kindness and faithfulness won't change and can't fail. True love is like that. It's dependable when everything else is unsure. Its loyalty isn't determined by our actions or our reciprocation. God's love for us is eternal without question or qualification, and it's here to greet us every morning and give us peace every night.

What are your favorite kindnesses in creation? Do you enjoy the miracle in every sunrise, the colors in a sunset, the smell of the magnolia, the cherry blossoms in spring, or the crisp, cool nights beneath a canopy of stars? Whatever it is that fills your heart with gratitude, savor it as often as you can. The kindnesses of God are everywhere, waiting to be noticed.

God could show you kindness by bringing you a cup of coffee every morning, just the way you like it. Instead, He's showing His kindness in the things He's already given. The people you love. The place you call home. The job you're gifted to do. The pet that makes you smile. The flowers you smell, the shade tree you sit under, or the sunrise you wake up to see. Psalm 143:8 can be our prayer today: "Let me see Your kindness to me in the morning, for I am trusting You. Show me where to walk, for my prayer is sincere." May our hearts agree with a resounding amen!

Dear God,

I'm grateful for Your kindness to me every morning and the countless ways You show it. Open my eyes to see and appreciate it more and more.

Keep Climbing

I'm sure now I'll see God's goodness in the exuberant earth. Stay with God! Take heart. Don't quit.

PSALM 27:13–14 THE MESSAGE

Some days we want to quit. *Everything.* We feel like sneaking away to a place where there are no demands to meet, no schedules to follow, and no responsibilities to fulfill. Our lives feel like they've become mountains of stress, worry, and too much to do, and we're climbing every day but getting no closer to where we want to be. Oh, what we wouldn't do to reach the summit, to see our hopes manifested, our goals met, and the life we've dreamed of in perfect view.

But we wake up every morning and *keep climbing*, because the journey is how we understand God's goodness. It's when we see Him most clearly and learn to trust Him fully, wildly, and *fiercely*. Take heart. *Don't quit.* Stay with God! The good things are going to outweigh the bad, and the *best* thing in life is getting to know Him when we reach the end of ourselves. We don't have answers to the whys or the whens, so we fall into His arms and surrender all.

That's when we know it's the only place we've truly wanted to be—close to Him, loved not because of our efforts or accomplishments but for the beauty of who we *are*. He'll never ask us to *be* more or to *do* more. Even on days when we fear His love won't hold on through the doubts, the failures, or our temptation to give up, His grip remains strong. God's love doesn't slack or let loose, and it *never* will.

When we wonder, the Bible answers, "I lift up my eyes to the mountains—where does my help come from? My help comes from the LORD, the Maker of heaven and earth. He will not let your foot slip—He who watches over you will not slumber" (Psalm 121:1–3 NIV). Our help is in place, our day is in motion, and our confidence is in the unstoppable love leading us upward.

Dear God,

Drawing closer to You is the highest calling of my life, and there's nothing more fulfilling. Give my heart a calm, steady trust in You.

Our True Mountain Guide

Be my safe leader, be my true mountain guide.
Free me from hidden traps; I want to hide
in You. I've put my life in Your hands. You
won't drop me, You'll never let me down.

PSALM 31:3–5 THE MESSAGE

It's hard to let go of the reins of our lives and trust God is holding them, guiding *every* aspect of our lives in the best direction. There are *so many* moving parts. Family, career, health, community, goals, dreams, and days overloaded with interruptions and the unexpected. Can God really keep track of everything going on in my life, when there are nearly *eight billion* people on earth? It's impossible to comprehend, and our words will forever fall short of describing Him.

C. S. Lewis wrote in that God "has infinite attention to spare for each one of us. He doesn't have to deal with us in the mass. You are as much alone with Him as if you were the only being He had ever created."* The proof of His presence is clear and constant not only in nature but in *every good thing* in our lives. Everything we have to be thankful for finds its source in God: "Whatever is good and perfect is a gift coming down to us from God our Father" (James 1:17 NLT).

God can be trusted with the details of our lives, and for the good that comes from every trial, the joy that emerges from the sorrow, and the hope that lights our way in the darkness. We *always* have His undivided attention. And thankfully, He sees what lies ahead of us, too, and faithfully orders our steps to avoid things that aren't in keeping with His purpose for us. When we rest in the love leading us forward, we can have peace in the moment we're in.

Life will challenge us to scale intimidating mountains, travel painful paths, and endure things we never thought we'd have to. But we have an almighty, able, and loving guide every inch of the way. We have grace sufficient enough to overcome any test on any day. And neither God nor grace will *ever* let us down.

Dear God,

Hold me in the strength of Your love and the power of Your grace. I'm peaceful today in the sure grip of Your hand.

* C. S. Lewis, *Beyond Personality: The Christian Idea of God* (New York: Macmillan, 1945), 16.

A Grown-Up Hiding Place

**He is a rugged mountain where I hide;
He is my Savior, a rock where none can
reach me, and a tower of safety.**

PSALM 18:2 TLB

Picture God as a tower you can walk into for some quiet time. The only thing you find there is silence and security. The world is held at bay and your heart is restful. The usual noise that fills your day is in the distance, and your mind begins to unclutter. Your spirit—the true you—lets out a huge sigh of relief. *God invites you to this place every day.*

Sometimes we need to physically be where nothing can reach us. We need a grown-up hiding place. It can be a corner of the backyard, a room in the house, or a special spot on our walking path. Any place that lets us step away from our ordinary obligations is a good hiding place. And God knows it's good for us. He created our bodies and minds to benefit from quiet time because it helps us get close to Him. It encourages reflection and a realization of what's most important in our lives. Often we come away with a new desire to reset our priorities.

God speaks to us in the quiet, too, because that's when our hearts can *really* listen. It's hard to hear Him in the nonstop coming, going, and doing of our days, when our phones are buzzing, our kids are tugging, or our workload is pressing. Alone time is the best time to let our hearts and minds dig deep for direction, decision-making, and divine wisdom. "If you want to know what God wants you to do, ask Him, and He will gladly tell you, for He is always ready to give a bountiful supply of wisdom to all who ask Him" (James 1:5 TLB).

Let God, our rugged mountain, be your spiritual hiding place today. Think of yourself climbing into His arms for a few moments of quiet. Let the stress fall away. Let Him relieve your racing mind, restore your run-down spirit, and recover your restful heart. Thankfully, God's amazing love is something we can *never* hide from.

Dear God,

You created my innermost being and built in me a need for quiet time with You. Give me wisdom in knowing when a break is necessary for my restoration and well-being.

God's Provision of Peace

So Abraham called that place The Lord Will Provide. And to this day it is said, "On the mountain of the Lord it will be provided."

GENESIS 22:14 NIV

Being in the mountains is peaceful, walking in a forest is energizing, sitting on the beach is soothing. Every moment spent in God's creation is *good for us.* Study after study is now proving it, but it was part of our Creator's plan from the beginning. It's free and freeing, and every part of our being is blessed by it. Time in nature is proven to reduce stress, clear our minds, increase our energy, and improve our mood.

It's worth the discipline to reap the rewards. When we take the time to enjoy and appreciate all God has given us for the health of our hearts, souls, and minds, we're exalting Him too. Psalm 150:6 says, "Let everything that has breath praise the Lord" (NIV). Praise reminds us that every breath we take comes from the One who gives life to everything in and on this amazing earth.

Thankfulness and praise bring restoration to the deepest parts of us. We become better at being at peace through tough situations. We feel more courageous and grounded when we have to do things that are challenging for us. We stay more focused on what's in front of us, having given our minds the chance to clear. God is the most loving provider, and the miracle of creation is a big part of His provision to us.

We shouldn't let a lot of days go by without getting outdoors, witnessing the wonder of nature, and inspiring our hearts to fill with praise at the beauty and glory in all that God has created. He inhabits our praises, there's fullness of joy in His presence, and His creation is *imbued* with things that are good for us. That's all the reason we need to make time in nature part of our routine.

Dear God,

I praise You for Your perfect and powerful provision for our well-being in all that You created. Your love surrounds us in the beauty of all we see.

God, it seems You've
been our home forever;
long before the
mountains were born,
Long before You brought
earth itself to birth,
from "once upon a time"
to "kingdom come"—
You are God.

PSALM 90:1–2 THE MESSAGE

Come with a Listening Ear

Come to Me with your ears wide open.
Listen, and you will find life.
ISAIAH 55:3 NLT

Often when we're alone, we feel grateful for the things that matter most to us. We're thankful for our relationships, the work we do, the communities we're a part of, and the homes we're blessed to live in. While that solitude encourages us to think about what we've already been given, it's also a time to open our hearts to what God has for us in the moment.

Going to God with appreciation and thankfulness is great for every part of us, and it's an important way to stay close to Him by being continually mindful of all the good things He gives. But when we spend time with Him, He wants us to come to Him with a listening ear too. He knows we need the powerful, life-giving words He gives in order to have peace, joy, and hope.

God will remind us that His strength is made perfect in our weakness, and with Him, *anything* is possible. He'll tell us, *Don't be afraid, I'm right here with you and I'm not going anywhere.* He'll whisper in a still, small voice, *I am going before you, I will not fail you. I love you with a love that has no bounds or conditions.* If we listen closely, He'll breathe life into our hearts' desires, help us conquer every fear, and renew our strength and courage. Abundant life is what God brings to our times of solitude, and our souls receive far more blessings than they could ever give in return.

When we leave quiet time with God in the back of our minds or at the bottom of our to-do lists, we miss out on a life-giving exchange that could make every area of our lives richer. Our spirits, souls, and bodies benefit from the strength God restores when we are alone with Him. If we view it as a priority and not a privilege saved for our less-busy days, we'll discover how necessary it is—and we'll be reminded how perfectly loved we are.

Dear God,

Help me see how important it is to come to You with open ears and a listening heart every day. Your love is my restoration and life.

Created with Love

God saw all that He had made,
and it was very good.

GENESIS 1:31 NIV

Time spent in "green space" is proven to have incredible health benefits. A simple walk through the woods or spending even twenty minutes every day outdoors can create a wellness ripple effect that has lasting benefits for our bodies and minds. Everything God made is good, and it's good for us to enjoy it.

The smell of trees and flowers, the sound of water and wind, the sight of sunbeams streaming through a forest canopy or a beautiful landscape—God created our senses to savor all the goodness in all He made. It's a wonderful way to sustain our peace of mind and combat the things that aren't so good.

God made provision for our well-being because He knew what was coming. He knew technology would race forward, the world would grow more complicated, and our lives would become far less simple. But His gentle love, sustaining grace, and calming, constant presence has not changed. He's always available, more than enough, and well able to uphold us no matter what we face at any time on any day.

The pace of the world makes it even more crucial to take advantage of the healing properties of God's creation. Away from the noise we find His nurturing presence in *all of nature*. His amazing love for us is evident, overwhelming, and breathtaking. Today, do what God asks you to do to reap all the astounding benefits: "Be glad; rejoice forever in My creation" (Isaiah 65:18 TLB).

Dear God,

I see Your goodness in nature and know the power of Your presence in every part of it. Thank You for meeting my need to relax, recharge, and restore peace to my heart and mind.

The Rule of Eight

I will both lie down in peace, and sleep; for You alone, O Lord, make me dwell in safety.

PSALM 4:8 NKJV

Without question we sleep better when we go to bed on a calm note—our minds peaceful and our worries silenced. There's a wise saying that employs the "rule of eight," eight words to remind us how to lie down in peace: "Give it to God and go to sleep." It's a great practice in letting go, being still, and knowing God is God and He doesn't need our help to carry the things that weigh us down.

Our days can feel long and stressful or smooth and peaceful, depending on our attitude, how much we relinquish to God, and how much pressure we put on ourselves. God wants to be part of it all: our mornings, our nights, our attitudes, our aspirations, and most of all, whatever's at the root of our fear and worry. He wants to pluck out every care we have and replace them with His *peace*.

There's truth for our attitude: "Be humble, thinking of others as better than yourself. . . . Your attitude should be the kind that was shown us by Jesus Christ" (Philippians 2:3, 5 TLB). There's truth for our aspirations: "Let us strip off every weight that slows us down . . . And let us run with endurance the race God has set before us" (Hebrews 12:1 NLT). There's truth for our fear: "Let Him have all your worries and cares, for He is always thinking about you and watching everything that concerns you" (I Peter 5:7 TLB).

No matter what life throws at us today, God will give us grace at the perfect pace. We don't have to be fearful about outcomes. We only have to trust the One who overcame the world for our peace of heart and mind. And if a care hangs on when we crawl into bed tonight, we'll give it to God and go to sleep.

Dear God,

My days and nights are in Your care. You know what's best, do what's best, and love me unconditionally. I have perfect peace knowing You make me dwell in safety.

Tender Care on Cloudy Days

Your steadfast love, O Lord, is as great as all the heavens. Your faithfulness reaches beyond the clouds.

PSALM 36:5 TLB

If today feels like it's going to be a cloudy, gloomy one, know that God is raining down His comfort and courage to get you through! Down days aren't defeated ones; they're a chance to let God hold us close and give us peace. It's okay to have rest and restoration days. It's okay to do whatever we have to do to feel rested and also to do nothing if we need to. Grace doesn't keep score, and there's no way we can deplete it. Its favor and forgiveness we can't earn or expend.

God's love and faithfulness reach beyond the clouds in the heavens, and they reach into our cloudy days. He understands everything we face more intimately than we realize. He knows every aspect of our intricate souls. We're unique. We handle things and feel things differently than anyone else. God is the only One who knows us well enough to give us what we need. He'll choose people to provide His care, and He'll move circumstances to prove His love, but His heart will be in perfect and precise control. We belong to Him, and He won't leave us longing for the tenderness we need.

As we take one grace-filled step after another, we can be confident God is the solid rock beneath our feet. Even when news shakes our stability and the trials of life rattle our courage, we can be braver still knowing we're firmly held in the hands of our Overcomer. There isn't a thing on earth or in the heavens that can shake Him, nor will there ever be. His faithful, fearless hold on us is the strength of our heart and our confidence forever.

Enjoy the peace of God today. Bask in His presence and rest in His love. Though storms bring dreary days, God gives the brightness of hope. In all things, His love prevails—and it's going to clear the way to what is beautiful and best.

Dear God,

Be my courage when I'm weary and my care when I'm weak. I know You're with me and working all the pieces into place. Give me the rest I need as I trust in You.

The Sweetest Joy

God's a safe-house for the battered, a sanctuary during bad times. The moment you arrive, you relax; you're never sorry you knocked.

PSALM 9:9–10 THE MESSAGE

It's worth it. Buy the dozen roses, make the quick stop at the park, slow down to admire the spring blossoms, eat the cake. We won't get the moments back. We can't put the thankfulness on hold. We have an opportunity to appreciate what's in front of us *right now*. The exact same moment, memory, and marvel will not come again. God offers countless gifts every single day that we hurry past and overlook. But He continues to give because He's the greatest giver, the perfect love, and the sweetest sanctuary. He's everything the world can't give us.

"It's with lasting love that I'm tenderly caring for you" (Isaiah 54:8 THE MESSAGE). God's love is never in a different place than where we are. Our life and His love are inseparable. His never-ending love surrounds us on every side and is revealed in every part of the natural world He created. Are we keeping our eyes and our hearts open to see it every day? His "I love yous" are constant!

Each one is precisely what we need, when we need it. It's up to us to look for them and to let them lift our spirits the way He planned for them to.

Divine gestures are not only the sweetest ones but also the strengthening ones. They affirm our worth and confirm His presence. They prove that every moment of our lives has His constant attention, and that He *knows* us. They're a surge of joy to our hearts and a simple hug for our world-weary souls. His love never leaves us alone to get through the hard days and long weeks. He's holding us and every care.

Open your eyes and heart *wide* today. God has little miracles of His love planned for us. Our life is His highest priority and His priceless possession. He sees us, and He's hoping we see the love in everything He sends.

Dear God,

My heart is filled with thankfulness for You. Your love is the safe place and sweetest joy of my life.

Dear Friend,

This book was prayerfully crafted with you, the reader, in mind. Every word, every sentence, every page was thoughtfully written, designed, and packaged to encourage you—right where you are this very moment. At DaySpring, our vision is to see every person experience the life-changing message of God's love. So, as we worked through rough drafts, design changes, edits, and details, we prayed for you to deeply experience His unfailing love, indescribable peace, and pure joy. It is our sincere hope that through these Truth-filled pages your heart will be blessed, knowing that God cares about you—your desires and disappointments, your challenges and dreams.

He knows. He cares. He loves you unconditionally.

BLESSINGS!
THE DAYSPRING BOOK TEAM